Co Londonderry

Edited by Steve Twelvetree

 Young**Writers**

First published in Great Britain in 2005 by:
Young Writers
Remus House
Coltsfoot Drive
Peterborough
PE2 9JX
Telephone: 01733 890066
Website: www.youngwriters.co.uk

SB ISBN 1 84602 117 0

Foreword

Young Writers was established in 1991 and has been passionately devoted to the promotion of reading and writing in children and young adults ever since. The quest continues today. Young Writers remains as committed to the fostering of burgeoning poetic and literary talent as ever.

This year's Young Writers competition has proven as vibrant and dynamic as ever and we are delighted to present a showcase of the best poetry from across the UK. Each poem has been carefully selected from a wealth of *Playground Poets* entries before ultimately being published in this, our thirteenth primary school poetry series.

Once again, we have been supremely impressed by the overall high quality of the entries we have received. The imagination, energy and creativity which has gone into each young writer's entry made choosing the best poems a challenging and often difficult but ultimately hugely rewarding task - the general high standard of the work submitted amply vindicating this opportunity to bring their poetry to a larger appreciative audience.

We sincerely hope you are pleased with our final selection and that you will enjoy *Playground Poets Co Londonderry* for many years to come.

Contents

Lauren Kyle (11)   20
Laura Bolton (10)   20

Gorran Primary School
Shane P Donnelly (9)   21
Lauren Smyth (10)   21
Philip McCullough (9)   22
Oliver Jamieson (9)   22
Tara Dempsey (9)   23
Jonathan Kane (9)   23
Shelly-Jo McClarty (10)   23
Mark Monahan (9)   24
Hannah Kennedy (9)   24
Gavin White (10)   25
Richard McNeill (9)   25
Jamie Leslie (8)   26
William Downs (9)   26
David Aiken (9)   27
Shannon White (10)   27
Dylan Leslie (10)   28

Longtower Primary School
Caoilin Healy (11)   29
Sean McGrory (10)   29
Steven McCallion (10)   30
Patrick McGrotty (11)   30

New Row Primary School
Nicole Johnston (10)   31
Ruairi Glavin (11)   31
Michael Gordon (11)   31
Bridie Maguire (11)   32
Ashley Johnston (11)   32
Alice Coogan (11)   33
Ross Gribben (11)   33
Matthew McNabb (10)   34
Stephen O'Hagan (10)   34
Cara Bell (10)   35
Órán Donnelly (10)   36
Joeleen Mullan (10)   36

Danielle Beatty (10)   37
Ryan O'Kane (11)   37
Nadine Lagan (10)   38

Portstewart Primary School
Adam Freeman (10)   38
Shannon Costello (10)   39
William Smyth (10)   39
Dillan Akyol (10)   40
Jenny Mitchell (10)   40
Tara Nicholl (10)   40
Christopher McNeill (11)   41
Andrew Lynch (11)   41
Lois Carson (10)   42
Natalie Costello (10)   42
Patrick Harris (10)   43
Richard Nicholl (10)   43
Daniel Burrough (10)   44
Rachel Millar (11)   44
Kheva Cole (10)   45
Gavin Darragh (11)   45
Hannah Bacon (10)   45
Leona Howarth (10)   46
Heather Spence (10)   47
Jane Walker (10)   48
Cristina Corbett (10)   49
Rebekah Moore (11)   49
Rebecca Patterson (10)   49
Emma Thompson (10)   50
Corey McDowell (10)   50
Jack Taggart (10)   51
Maeve Hough (10)   51
Christopher Coils (11)   51
Daniel Burns (10)   52
Jordan Hemphill (11)   52
Casandra Patton (10)   52
Ross Wakefield (11)   53
Megan Nelson (11)   53
Owen McKinney (11)   54
Ben Porter (11)   54
Rachel Wilson (11)   55

Ashleigh Evans (10)   56
Carolanne McGowan (10)   57
Marcus Galbraith (11)   57
Aaron Fielding (10)   58

St Canice Primary School, Dungiven
Shannon O'Kane (10)   58
Sinéad O'Connor (9)   59
Erin McGuigan (10)   59
Brid McCloskey (10)   60
Justine Doherty (9)   60
Conor McCloskey (10)   61
Shauna Craig (10)   61
Eilish McLaughlin (10)   62
Niall O'Kane (9)   62
Michael Brolly (9)   63
Aoife Hannon (10)   63
Lorraine McNicholl (9)   64
Ciara McLaughlin (9)   64
Conall Mallon (9)   65

St Colmcilles Primary School, Claudy
Niall Devine (8)   65
Marie-Clare Devine (9)   66
Karen McGlinchey (10)   66
Caoimhe O'Neill (10)   67
Serena McElhinney (8)   67
Emmet O'Kane (9)   67
Jodie Carlin (9)   68
Michelle McKeever (7)   68
Aaron Donaghy (9)   69
Martin Brolly (8)   69
Aine McCloskey (10)   70
Fionain Smyth (9)   70
Conor Doherty (8)   70
Colleen Ward (8)   71
Cathal O'Reilly (8)   71
Loren Ward (8)   72
Shane Brown (9)   72
Maria Kelly (10)   73
Cathal O'Neill (9)   73

Megan Farren (8)	74
Ciaran McCloskey (10)	74
Ethan Browne (7)	74
Jordan Hone (9)	75
Emma McCloskey (8)	75
Aileen Burke (8)	75
Naomi Martin (7)	76
Sean Curran (8)	76
Paidi Donaghy (7)	76
Emily Clayton (7)	77
Kevin Ward (10)	78
Erin O'Kane (8)	78
Shauna McCloskey (8)	78
Shaune Gormley (8)	79
Ellen Hendron (8)	79
Fintan Gormley (7)	79
Laura Duffy (8)	80
Megan Harkin (9)	80
Connor Bradley (8)	80
Niall Logue (9)	81

St John's Primary School, Swatragh

Niamh Quigg (9)	81
Clodagh McKeefry (10)	82
Lauren Elliott (7)	82
Aine O'Kane (7)	82
Kate McKeefry (7)	83
Catherine McCloy (7)	83
Cathy Harkin (7)	83
John Quigg (11)	84
Eimear Browne (7)	84
Patrick Turner (7)	84
Sean Dillon (7)	85
Peadar Coyle (7)	85
John McCormack (7)	85
Bronagh McKeefry (10)	86
Eimear Cassidy (7)	86
Stephen Coyle (10)	87
Claire McGuigan (10)	87
Victoria Lagan (7)	88
Aimee McQuillan (8)	88

Eiméar O'Kane (10)	89
Eileen Quigg (8)	89
Sara Dillon (10)	90
Bronagh McKeown (9)	90
Rachel Donnelly (10)	91
Aimee Harkin (9)	91
Anna Shiels (9)	92
Ryan Crawford (9)	92
Rebecca McKeefry (9)	92
Aisling McMullan (11)	93
Phillip Convery (8)	93
Ciaran Lagan (8)	94
Mark Mellon (9)	94
John Walsh (7)	94
Sarah Quigg (11)	95
Cathal Quinn (8)	95
Emma McPeake (10)	96
Aoife Coyle (9)	96
Rebecca Lagan (10)	97
Niamh McEldowney (10)	97
Danielle McKeefry (10)	98
Thomas O'Hagan (11)	98
Catherine McCloskey (11)	99
John Joe Quigg (10)	99
Ciara Browne (9)	100
Sean Quinn (9)	100
Patrick Lagan (9)	100
Kathryn Mullan (9)	101

St Mary's Primary School, Maghera

Cathair Glass (8)	101
Enda Gallagher (9)	101
Luke Fullerton	102
Jude Doherty (8)	102
Shannon Burke (9)	102
Conor Convery (9)	103
Gavin Toner (9)	103
Ciaran McCloy (9)	103
Maeve Morren (11)	104
Ciaran O'Hagan (9)	104
Bronagh McGuckin (8)	105

Shane Turner (8)	105
Niamh McFalone (9)	106
Una Dowdall (11)	106
Meghan Irwin (10)	107
James Grant (10)	107
Karl Quinn (9)	108
Aine Craig (11)	108
Thomas McErlean (11)	108
Aidan McCoy (10)	109
Joanne Eppleston (11)	109
Niamh Ledgewood (8)	109
Shauna McCloskey (9)	110
Shea Leyden (9)	110
Aiden McGrath (9)	110
Nuala Convery (11)	111
Kim McFalone (8)	111
Sean McIlvenny (9)	111
Shea Gribbon (9)	112
Piaras Flanagan (8)	112
Charlotte Burke (8)	112
Kerry Johnson (9)	113
Sarah Grant (9)	113
Gary Cunningham (8)	113

St Paul's Primary School, Slievemore

Paul Stewart (11)	114
Nicole McCloskey (10)	114
Bobbie-Leigh Kelly (9)	115
Caolan Robinson (8)	115
Liam McDevitt (9)	116
Dayle King (9)	116
Alisha Belgrave (11)	117
Aoife Curran (8)	117
Shauna-Marie Stanway (11)	118
David Houston (8)	118
Arón Halsey (11)	119
Aaron Robinson (10)	119
Patrick Quigley (10)	120
Kevin Harrison (8)	120
Denise Coyle (10)	121
Rachel Kelly (10)	122

Termoncanice Primary School

Rebecca Henry (9)   141
Thea McCloskey (9)   142
Ryan Campbell (9)   142
Chloe Pearson (9)   142
Amyleigh O'Connor (9)   143
Niamh Feeney (9)   143
Nicole McGillion (9)   143
Daniel Forrest (9)   144
Saoirse Mullan (9)   144
Ruairi Hassan (9)   145
Correy Feeney (9)   145
Lewis Donaghy (9)   146
Catherine Carlin Moore (9)   146
Rosie Forrest (8)   146
Roisin Turner (9)   147
Alice McGee (9)   147
Matthew Simpson (8)   147
Aaron Mullan (9)   148
Maria McQuillan (8)   148
Seamus O'Hara (9)   149
Mark Gormley (9)   149
Conor Murphy (9)   150
Aoife Murray (9)   150
Blaine Ferris (8)   151
Paul McLaughlin (9)   151

Trench Road Primary School
Stephen McDermott (10)   151
Eve Hinds (10)   152
Danielle Moran (10)   152
Dearbháile McKinney (11)   152
Sophie Moore (11)   153
Joseph McDermott (10)   153
Jane Doherty (10)   153
Kevin Harkin (9)   154
Dearbhla Tunney (9)   154
Bronagh Brolly (9)   155
Sinead Meenan (11)   155
Siofra Coyle (11)   155
Enya McGlinchey (9)   156

The Poems

Back At School

When I went back
Things had changed,
Everything was rearranged,
Got a new teacher,
Tables had changed.

New pupils had come,
There'll be new friends
To play with at break time
And learn more games.

I have to catch up
With the work I missed,
It's amazing what happens
In just one week.

Colleen Bradley (9)
Bunscoil Cholmcille Primary School

Changes In School

When I went back
Nothing was the same.
My teacher had changed,
What a shame!

Even my friend changed her name
From Sarah to Sorcha,
I felt on my own,
I wish I could just go home.

Coming to Friday,
I just couldn't wait
To get off school again
And play with my mate.

Brídín Nic Cionnaith (9)
Bunscoil Cholmcille Primary School

Back To School

When I went back
Nothing was the same.
New games, new pupils,
New rules,
Life isn't the same.

Pupils with strange names,
We're all learning new games.
The work is getting harder,
I can't understand it.

Life is moving on,
We're making new friends.
Games are getting harder
Like hopscotch and line-tag.

Brónagh Houston (9)
Bunscoil Cholmcille Primary School

I Went Back

Back after being sick,
Everything was different,
Nothing would click.

Everyone knew more than I did,
I really just thought
I should have gone and hid.

At last I was picked,
First again.
Everything was better
From then on in.

Aaron Ó Fearraigh (9)
Bunscoil Cholmcille Primary School

What's Really Different

School has changed,
I feel deranged,
Our teacher seems crazy,
I feel tired and hazy.

New pupils and games,
Hard to pronounce some names,
Pupils from Africa, Scotland,
Portugal and England.

Dawning of a new,
I feel less like a dart,
Made some new friends,
Hey, I'm fitting in.

Shannon Downey (10)
Bunscoil Cholmcille Primary School

New School

Back to school, nothing the same,
Old teachers have gone, new have come,
I'm feeling left out,
I wish I had never come.

Work is hard,
Children are confused,
Teachers want to be amused.
Work is over for today, now we can go and play.

Made a friend called Lux Sing,
Stayed in the playground
Until I heard the bell ring.
Another friend called Chim Po, I got to fit in.

Ciarán Ó Corráin (9)
Bunscoil Cholmcille Primary School

School Days

School is different, nothing is the same,
My old teacher is gone, my new teacher is here.
There are new students and new games,
Everyone knows more than me.

Every time I try to do my work
I can't even think or even blink.
There is a new office,
The playground has more people.

My belly hurts,
I tell my teacher, he thinks it's a trick
But I still feel sick,
Wish I was in my warm bed.

Caolán Kinsella (10)
Bunscoil Cholmcille Primary School

Back To School

Back to school,
Nothing was the same,
New rules, new games,
New teachers, new work.
Why did I come back?
Harder work, harder to understand.
Strange children are playing
Games I don't understand.

The principal is kind,
Homework is difficult,
Maths is harder,
School is the best place to be.

Róisín Wilson (9)
Bunscoil Cholmcille Primary School

Back To School

Back after being sick,
My teacher had gone, another had come,
My friends went away, I have to stay.

Rules changed, no chips at all
And no one is allowed to play with a ball.
Our logo has changed but it is just the picture.

I'm fitting in with changes
But I can't find a friend
That can make me grin.

Gráinne Ní Chearúill (9)
Bunscoil Cholmcille Primary School

Cool School!

School is cool,
I love netball,
Like volleyball,
Hate football,
Learn hockey,
Enjoy golf,
Adore gymnastics!

School is cool,
I doodle at drawing,
Splash at painting,
Rush at colouring,
Think of designs,
Scribble at art!

School is cool,
In class I'm talking,
At break time I'm laughing,
In assembly I'm singing,
In PE we're listening,
Mess at reading!

Lois Colgan (10)
Castledawson Primary School

Fun In School

Paint comes in a variety of colours
And I like sharing that beauty with others.
But when you're starting to plan it out,
Have you got your pencil about?

Music is something everyone likes,
But when it's over everyone goes home on their bikes.
When you get home it's time to revise,
It's 8am so I'm back in the teacher's eyes.

PE is enjoyable to do
Because you never know what game to do.
There's a choice between
Football and basketball,
But where's the football
And where's the basketball?

Danielle Anderson (9)
Castledawson Primary School

School Is Fun

At break and dinner
We run and get thinner.
School is great,
We have to make our own fate.
School is fun,
We are not allowed toy guns.
At the canteen
Some people get buns.
While we eat our buns
We sit on our bums.
The teachers are nice,
At lunch some people get rice.
On trips we go on ice.
When we play snake
We throw a dice
And that is the end of school!

Jade Kennedy (11)
Castledawson Primary School

Young Writers - Playground Poets Co Londonderry

Footy

Shooting is an important skill,
But kit and boots are better,
The ball would be leather,
The stadium could have five floors.
Our team are spectacular on the grassy pitch,
But then the nets are really big,
So we're lucky we have a classy keeper.

Supporters cheer when a goal is scored,
Players dribble down the pitch to score a goal.
Then a centre kick is taken,
But if they kick before the referee blows his whistle
The opposition gets a free kick.

Subs come on when a player gets injured
Or if a team is getting stuffed five-nil.
If a man is fouled in the box the team he plays for gets a penalty.
At half-time the players go off,
The manager gives a good, encouraging team talk.
If a team wins
The players go off the pitch running
And clapping like nobody's business.

Robert Wallace (10)
Castledawson Primary School

Super School

Painting, painting is fun,
Drawing, drawing I love it too,
Sketching, sketching can be hard,
Shading, shading makes my picture look better,
Planning, planning gives me an idea what to do.

Violins, violins make a lovely sound,
Tin whistles, tin whistles make a lovely sound too,
Notes, notes sometimes are hard to learn,
Songs, songs are lovely,
Recorders, recorders I like them too.

PE kits, PE kits we change into them for PE,
Horses, horses I love jumping over you,
Climbing bars, climbing bars I like them too,
Gymnastics, gymnastics I like so,
Netball, netball it's okay.

School plays, school plays I love to do,
Actions, actions are sometimes hard,
Dressing up, dressing up is fun,
Singing, singing is okay,
Learning words, learning words is not fun.

What a week at school!

Amy Stanley (10)
Castledawson Primary School

PE

PE is fun,
PE is healthy,
PE is fit.

Netball is fun,
Netball is all about having exercise,
There is a centre, wing attack,
Wing defence, goalkeeper and goal scorer.
You can throw the ball,
You can jump,
Netball is fun.

Football is fit,
Football is all about enjoying yourself,
You can have free kicks, corners, penalties, fouls and goals,
You can kick the ball and head the ball,
The goalkeeper tries to save
And you pass to each other.

Volleyball is enjoyable,
Volleyball is all about having fun,
You can hit the ball,
you can serve the ball over the big high net,
Everyone just loves it.

I love PE.

Carly Young (11)
Castledawson Primary School

Sports

Basketball is fun,
But now when you fall on your bum.
I pass to Jade,
She shoots the ball.
I pass to Ross,
He dribbles up and across.

Football is fun,
I pass to Jade,
She scores like a gun.
I pass to Michaela,
She scores penalties
And free kicks.

Netball is fun,
But now when you fall on your bum.
I pass to Jade, she scores a goal,
She did a wee flippy and landed on the floor.
I like to win
A nice silver tin.

PE is fun,
I throw a ball,
It goes like a gun.
I kick a ball, it goes very slow,
I have a gang, come on let's go.

Carlene McLeish (11)
Castledawson Primary School

School Is Fun!

School is time for fun and games,
Everyone loves football,
Basketball is fun,
Girls play netball,
Primary 4 and 5 play tig,
We go on computers,
I like working at geography,
I like maths but not many people do,
People prefer English and I like it too!

I like PE like everyone else,
Drawing is my favourite, of course,
Playing with friends is what most people do,
We learn to play hockey during PE,
We like to go on trips,
We talk and we talk, no time to stop,
We paint 'til our hands are dirty,
I try to think of designs!

At break time we play,
At lunchtime we sing,
We learn to play golf,
I like to colour-in,
I like to run and jump,
I like writing,
The teachers are nice,
Sports day is cool,
We learn gymnastics,
We like to giggle,
I like to laugh,
School is fun!

Lauren Smyth (11)
Castledawson Primary School

School Is Great!

School is great,
Well most of it anyway.
You get to meet new friends
And most importantly
Play footy break and dinner.

Computers, amazingly advanced through the years
And we get free Internet from eight to six.
Yeah
Like I said
School is great.

We get trophies,
They are class,
We go to England sometimes.
Like I said
School is great.

PE, deadly but fun,
You lose your breath,
You lose your pounds.
Like I said
School is great.

Tutu you also get music,
You never know,
Maybe you could be in a pop group.
Like I said
School *is great*.

David Sampson (11)
Castledawson Primary School

Nothing Can Beat Playing

A full week of school,
How busy it can be,
It's good when half-term comes,
When the playground we'll see.

It doesn't matter what sport we play
You're sure to score at least one goal,
Penalties and hat-tricks, dribbling the ball,
Yes you've guessed it, it's *football!*

Tackling and passing, using your skill,
Because of course you're going to need skill in football.
Team against team, dribbling the ball,
You hear a big cheer, you've scored a goal!

There's no point walking about looking so bored,
Don't waste time netball is waiting,
Your team is waiting to pass to you,
Your team succeeds because you're playing too!

The basketball net is deserted and dusty,
But the cobwebs have gone,
It's all down to a gust of wind,
Flown from the kids so fond!

'Who's taking centre?' we always ask,
'I will!' 'And I will too!' is what we'll hear,
The ball goes up and the passing begins,
In no time at all we'll know who wins!

The bell rings, it's time to hit the books,
Maths and English
And history too,
But in no time at all the playground we see once again!

Rebecca Finlay (9)
Castledawson Primary School

Football Crazy

If you are a supersub
You will score lots of goals,
You will be like Ronaldhino
Or Ronaldo with an overhead kick.

Watch you don't hit the crossbar
Or put it over either,
We are trying to put it in the bottom corner.

Stevie G and Milan B usually dribble
And score a good goal in the top corner
Or maybe the bottom,
You just don't know where that ball's going to go!

If you're at a Liverpool match
You will hear the supporters sing,
'You'll Never Walk Alone,'
Or if Milan Baros scores
They shout, 'Milan . . . Milan.'

The captain is the man who tells you what to do,
The manager is the man who is in charge of the crew.

Gareth Steele (10)
Castledawson Primary School

Teachers!

My teacher is strict but rather nice;
Her class can be quiet as mice.
If we should start a fight,
Our punishment might not be light.
During her lessons we have to concentrate,
Otherwise she may keep us in late.
Our teacher works us very hard all day
Just to earn her pay.
So I would suggest please reduce her pay,
Then her pupils could just relax and play.

Jonathan Kyle (9)
Culnady Primary School

Darkness

Darkness is like a black colour.
It sounds like a big ghost through the air.
It tastes like cold, spooky blood.
It smells like warm, dirty blood.
It looks like a dark sky ready to close in.
It feels like dirty, smelly blood from a ghost.
It reminds me of the dark sky at night.

Kyle Moore (8)
Culnady Primary School

Snow

Snow is falling from the sky,
Now you can eat a mince pie,
Off you go in the snow,
Snow is falling very low,
Many people outside,
Always wrap up warm,
Now it is time for the snow to go.

Hannah Bolton (10)
Culnady Primary School

My Farm

M y farm is great.
Y ou can feed the animals.

F arming is good fun.
A ll the animals run around and around.
R ide the horses around the field.
M y farm is messy.

Sarah Porter (10)
Culnady Primary School

Summer

Summer is a time to play,
Go on your holidays in May,
Into the swimming pool,
When you are on holidays there is no rule.

On to the slide
And away you go,
When will it ever end,
You don't know.

Lots of people are playing on the slide,
Then off the diving board somebody glides,
Sitting on an inflatable boat,
On this activity you don't need your coat.

Andrea Connell (9)
Culnady Primary School

My Dog

M y dog is the best ever,
Y ou could never get a better dog.

D ogs are all I like,
O ther people say that it is stupid but I say it is the
G reatest dog ever.

Heather Irwin (9)
Culnady Primary School

Hallowe'en

Hallowe'en is spooky,
Witches, wizards flying about,
Everybody scared to death,
Having parties for a laugh,
I have never been so scared in my life,
I cannot believe I have been so, so scared in my life.

Michael Scott (9)
Culnady Primary School

Multi Poem!

There are some poems that I've made up,
Here is one or two.
With no regard
It's really hard,
Here is one for you!

There was a wee tractor called Frank
Who pulled a big slurry tank.
While crossing a river
He went into a shiver,
And fell in the water
And sank!

Here's another one,
It sounds like it is fun.

There was once a dog called Holly
Who went for a ride in a trolley.
She shouted out, 'Wheeeeee!'
Then banged into a tree.
Then I just thought, *what a wally!*

Timothy Kelso (10)
Culnady Primary School

Happiness

Happiness is the colour pink like blossoms falling from the trees,
Happiness sounds like my heart beating with love,
Happiness tastes like the sweet of the day,
Happiness smells like a flower rising from the ground,
Happiness looks like the sun setting,
Happiness feels wonderful and exciting like a snowflake falling
                                                    from the sky.
Happiness reminds me of my friends Hannah, Laura and Andrea.

Hannah Irwin (10)
Culnady Primary School

I Love The Seasons

Spring
God's beautiful work of art,
Gives everything a new start,
Colours, sounds, sights, whatever could be better?

Summer
The beach comes in with this season,
I do love the beach for four reasons,
Sun, sea, shells, stones, all so beautiful.

Autumn
The woods covered in carpets of leaves,
The fields with corn in their sheaves,
Leaves, trees, shorter days best of all.

Winter
Short, cold and frosty days,
Out in the snow the children play,
Snow, school holidays, Christmas, my favourite time of year!

I love the seasons!

Grace Kelso (8)
Culnady Primary School

Friends

Friends are kind,
Friends are sweet,
Sometimes share,
Sometimes stare.
Friends fight,
But that's alright
'Cause in the end
They're still our friends,
They're always there,
They always care.

Andrea Cochrane (9)
Culnady Primary School

Susie

Susie is my dog,
She is my special friend,
I love the way she wags her tail
And sniffs to say hello.

We chase the ball and play,
We do it every day,
We walk along the lane,
We always play so many games.

She is an English springer,
She is also liver and white,
She wears a brown collar
And has a big brown patch on one eye.

Susie loves her ball,
She comes when I call,
She loves to splash in streams,
Susie you're the answer to my dreams.

Sarah Mulholland (11)
Culnady Primary School

Friendship

Friends have good times together
With laughter, smiles and fun
And even when times are bad
You know you're not alone.

You probably will fall out
Every once in a while,
But forgive and forget
And you'll soon start to smile!

Caring, fun and sharing
That's what friends are for
And to set you right again
Whenever you go wrong!

Amy Conway (10)
Culnady Primary School

What's On The Menu?

Chips with fish
What a dish.
Chocolate and jelly
Upsets your belly.

Chicken and pork
Eaten with a fork.
Cream and milk
Down our throats like silk.

Eggs with raw meat
That no one would eat.
Curry and rice
That sounds nice.

Pepper and chilli
Turns you silly.
To finish a salad
I must be totally mad.

Lauren Kyle (11)
Culnady Primary School

Happiness

Happiness is all different colours,
It sounds like a lovely piano playing peaceful tunes,
It tastes like a juicy strawberry,
It smells like fresh flowers,
It looks like a sparkly rainbow all around me,
It makes you feel jolly and jumpy,
It reminds me of my *wonderful* friends,
Hannah Irwin, Andrea Connell
And Hannah Bolton.

Laura Bolton (10)
Culnady Primary School

The Concert

One day my mum said,
'Come on there's a concert in town!'
I got up, put on my flippers,
Instead of my slippers,
I brushed my hair with a slimy bone
Instead of a comb.
I got dressed
Putting my pyjamas back on,
We went to the concert,
Right in a flash,
We got to the concert
But that was a big mistake!
People started to laugh at me,
It was such a drag!
But hey! I was up on stage,
My heart went crazy,
Especially when I saw Aunty Mazy
And all of that never would have happened
If I had just taken my time!

Shane P Donnelly (9)
Gorran Primary School

Pets

I like dogs because they lick you
And roll over for you.
I like cats because they purr
And sit at your feet.
I like rabbits because they are soft
And always hop.
I like fish because they are nice
When they swim.
But overall the best so far is a parrot,
It will talk to you when you're lonely.

Lauren Smyth (10)
Gorran Primary School

Chelsea V Arsenal

Chelsea V Arsenal,
What a game!
Arjen Robben's taking aim,
He shoots to the left,
Almunia dives to the right,
Arjen Robben runs with delight,
Now 1-0 is the score!
And Chelsea want more!

Half-time!
'Good play lads,
You've done me and the crowd proud!
Well what can I say, just play the same
And you're sure to win!'

Full-time!
'Brilliant play lads, 3-0.'

Philip McCullough (9)
Gorran Primary School

The Unicorn

The unicorn is a gentle animal,
Its lovely streaming white mane,
Its long silver tail.

When a storm takes place in the forest
It gallops through the puddles,
If it was in a race it would win first prize.

When it finds shelter
It walks around a bit,
Then it settles down to rest.

Oliver Jamieson (9)
Gorran Primary School

Busted

B usted! Today, the dreaded day has arrived, too soon for me!
The big question is - are Busted going to split up? No one knows!
U nder a question mark they must be, so many questions by their
manager. He must have pleaded with them not to split!
S o will they or not? Who will know? It will be on the news!
T he fans go mad saying, 'Oh imagine a world with no Busted!'
E veryone hurries home for the five o'clock news. 'Shhhh!' says my
mum. Busted went bust, all the fans cry with sadness!
D own in the dumps I was . . . until I heard McFly were back in town!

Tara Dempsey (9)
Gorran Primary School

Friends

F or friends I would do anything, even stick my head in the fireplace
as long as there was no fire.
R obert is my best friend from my old school.
I like having friends a lot.
E very day I see friends, it's fun to play with them.
N ow I would like to say that friends are the best.
D ylan sits opposite me, I play his games at break.
S ome of my friends I like better than others but they are
all my friends.

Jonathan Kane (9)
Gorran Primary School

Kittens

K ittens are cute and furry.
I n the barn they hide and hunt for mice.
T hey climb up your leg and the claws go in.
T hey lick your face and fingers.
E very time I call 'Babies' they come running to my feet.
N ever would they bite me.
S ometimes they can be bad but I love them and that is what matters.

Shelly-Jo McClarty (10)
Gorran Primary School

My Mum And Dad

I love my mum with all my might,
I love when she makes me tea,
I love when she takes me on holidays
To get away from school days.
I love when she looks after me
When I have a sore tummy.
My mum is great!

I love my dad with all my might,
I love when he plays with me,
We play football and things like that,
He takes me to all sorts of matches.
I think my dad is great!

But most of all I love them both the same!

Mark Monahan (9)
Gorran Primary School

If The World Was Made Of Sugar

If the world was made of sugar
Wouldn't it be great?
You could eat anything,
Like the clouds and the trees.

The flowers would be made of candy,
The clouds would be made of candyfloss,
And the streets would be made of chocolate,
And houses would be made of sweets.

Just wouldn't it be great
If the world was made of sugar,
Just so nice,
Just so nice,
If the world was made of sugar.

Hannah Kennedy (9)
Gorran Primary School

Little Dragon

There was a little dragon
And it had fiery breath,
Its mummy was very ill,
Then she came to her death.

So then the little dragon
Was left all alone,
But then his daddy
Died and he had no home.

So then the little dragon
Went to find a home,
But when he couldn't
Find one he started to moan.

Then he saw a little house
And thought he could find a mum,
So he went to the door
And a mummy dragon said, 'We have a son!'

So the little dragon went in
And told them about his mum.
He started to cry and they said,
'You are the best son!'

Gavin White (10)
Gorran Primary School

Crisps

C risps are the best in the world.
R eally good crisps.
I like salt and vinegar,
S o what flavour do you like?
P ackets of crisps in my tummy,
S o why don't you buy some.

Richard McNeill (9)
Gorran Primary School

The Big Match

Arsenal and Man U
Are playing each other.
So far it is nil-nil.
Here is Reyes,
He passes it
To Henry,
He shoots, oooh it's over
The bar.
Goooooal!

It is half-time.

They're on again,
Bergkamp runs up
The wing.
Roy Keane
Comes up and hacks
Bergkamp.
Roy Keane is red-carded!
Bergkamp is off!
Henry takes a free kick.

He kicks it and it goes
In the back of the net.
Goooooal!

Jamie Leslie (8)
Gorran Primary School

Brum! Brum!

Twin cams are flying,
Brum! Brum!
Twin cams are drifting sideways,
Brum! Brum!
Twin cams are flying down the motorway,
Brum! Brum!
But most of all twin cams are cooooool!

William Downs (9)
Gorran Primary School

Man U V Chelsea

It was the day that
Man United were playing Chelsea.
They were in the changing room
And the Chelsea team
Were drinking pints of beer.
Will they be able to play?
I don't know, it's time
To start the match.
They run out,
Man U are taking centre.
Who will win?
They kick off,
Then Chelsea are
Falling on top
Of everyone.
The referee comes out,
He says, 'Man U have won!'

David Aiken (9)
Gorran Primary School

Debbie

Oh how I wish I had long nails like Debbie!
I wish I was tall like Debbie!
Debbie is sweet, kind and nice.
She's brilliant at cooking
And has lovely short hair.
I have short hair but not like hers.

She has blue eyes that sparkle in the night,
I've seen them!

And her name sounds better than . . .
Soda ice cream fruit drinks with ice shaped as stars!

Shannon White (10)
Gorran Primary School

FA Cup Final 2005

It's the FA Cup final, Man U versus CFC,
The captains shake hands, *kick off!*
Gudjohnsen does a back pass to Robben,
Robben is running up the wing in the box,
Foul! Penalty given to Chelsea,
Robben steps up, takes it, *goal!*
Alex Ferguson is raging about the penalty,
Ronaldo makes a breakthrough, *Ronaldo,*
What a save by Petr Cech!
Drogba has made a pass to Lampard, shoots, *goal!*
The pressure's on Alex Ferguson,
What a volley by Ryan Giggs!
Over the bar,
2 more minutes until it's half-time,
Oh another goal by Chelsea,
3-0 to CFC!
Man U pass the ball to Scholes,
Now Keane shoots.
Save! Rebound! *Goal!* by Wayne Rooney, 3-1!
Scholes has been fouled! Free kick!
That's a well-taken free kick, *goal!*
Ronaldo hits the ball from 65 yards out,
Over the keeper in the top corner, *goal!*
3-3, one more goal needed,
Louis Saha has been fouled, looks bad,
Red card for John Terry!
Nistelrooy is on for Saha,
Nistelrooy! Goal! Last minute winner!
Alex Ferguson is waaayyy over happy.
Man U FA Cup winners 2005!

Dylan Leslie (10)
Gorran Primary School

Through My Eyes

Through my eyes I can see . . .
A hummingbird, a bumblebee,
Footballers in the football field,
A fisherman pulling in his reel.

Through my eyes I can see . . .
My baby brother looking at me,
Laughing and giggling up at me,
Oh I'm so glad that's what I see.

Through my eyes I can see . . .
Mrs Burk beside me,
She tells me how to spell,
When I'm stuck she's the one I tell.

Through my eyes I can see . . .
My poem is finished,
Yippee.

Caoilin Healy (11)
Longtower Primary School

I Wish . . .

I wish for the moon and the stars
And a hundred Milky Bars.
I wish for piles of money and lots of honey,
But it's awfully runny.

I wish for gold and silver
And a boat to go down a river.
I wish to fly, soaring by
And saying to people hello and hi.

I wish I could swim across the Pacific,
It would be really terrific.
I wish I had a dinosaur friend,
People would think I'm round the bend.

Sean McGrory (10)
Longtower Primary School

I Wish . . .

I wish I had a dog
With a great big tail.
I wish it had big teeth
To bite intruders when they come.

I wish I had lots of money,
I'd buy a boat and bars
And maybe game stores,
Maybe the world to see.

I wish I was 18
Then I'd be allowed to drive.
I'd have a place to myself,
I'd work hard every day so that would be good.

I wish I was strong
Then I would be feared by all.
Nobody would bully me
And I wouldn't bully them.

Steven McCallion (10)
Longtower Primary School

I Wish I Had Everything

I wish I had everything, I wish I had you!
I wish I could bark, I wish I could coo!
I wish that we would never grow old!
I wish it was always warm and never cold!

I wish I had everything, even the moon,
I'd make an eclipse - people will say it's doom!
I wish I had a mansion - a hut of logs,
I wish I could transform into breeds of dogs!

Patrick McGrotty (11)
Longtower Primary School

Death Is Here

Death is here,
I can smell it in the night.
I hear people bawl and shout as their loved ones pass away.
We sleep in our raggy clothes.
Oh, what's that what I hear?
I'm going to see what has happened.
'What's wrong?'
'Bridget's gone forever,' my mother wails.
Goodbye my precious Bridget.

Nicole Johnston (10)
New Row Primary School

The Awful Killer

I'm watching on the hill -
What an atrocious sight.
People going around in carts
Collecting dead people by the dozen,
Taking them to that awful place down the road.
I'm wondering if that will kill me some time
Or will I make it through this awful killer?
Only time will tell!

Ruairi Glavin (11)
New Row Primary School

The Famine

Many people have wondered
Why the famine struck Ireland.
I often ask myself the same question.
I wonder if I too will someday be lying
In the bushes alongside the road.
I do not have any food or water
I fear that soon I will perish.

Michael Gordon (11)
New Row Primary School

On The Road To Castletaggart!

It was dreadful!
No food, *no* water.
I fear we're going to die!
We are dragging ourselves along . . .
. . . My family are getting weaker . . .
. . . We're never going to make it . . .
The appalling smell of death is just around the corner.
I pray that we are not the next victims of this unrelenting killer -
No!
I know we will make it
If our spirit remains strong
And we place our trust in the
Almighty one!

Bridie Maguire (11)
New Row Primary School

The Famine Is Here

What is wrong?
What is it?
Oh no!
You must be joking!
The famine is here!
Are we going to die
Or will we make it to another day?
Oh no! Oh please God
Just let death pass over me.
Please God, spare us this awful fate
Before it is too late.

Ashley Johnston (11)
New Row Primary School

Death's Chant

Death raises his rotted arms,
Death flexes his skeletal fingers,
Death lifts his hooded head,
Death is shrouded in despair as he chants,

'The Irish they are suffering,
The potatoes they are rotting,
The fever it is growing,
The death rate, rising steadily.'

Death throws back his disguised head,
Death lets out an evil cackle,
Death raises his putrid arms once more,
Death, in the darkness, vanishes.

Alice Coogan (11)
New Row Primary School

My Dad's Spacecraft

My dad's spacecraft
Gave us many a laugh.
One day we took to space
And we saw a UFO,
But we were too slow,
As it went by shouting, 'Ho, ho, ho!'
But on the way home
I wrote a poem.
Do you want to hear it . . . ?
. . . Well you just did!

Ross Gribben (11)
New Row Primary School

Black

Black is like the night sky
High above the ground.
Is there anything up there?
Maybe. Maybe not.
As I lie in bed I often wonder
If there is anything up there.
I know that I won't find out until I get there!

Black is like the cats striding through the night,
You'd better watch out for our wild friends
Whose eyes we only see!
Remember to be careful
Or they might just give you a fright!

Matthew McNabb (10)
New Row Primary School

My Hero

My hero is like a bolt of lightning
Drifting through the night sky.
My hero is as sly as a fox
Sneaking up on their enemies.
My hero is as strong as an ox
Fighting an entire army.
My hero is as smart as
A super computer.
My hero is so bright
He lights up my world.

My hero is my dad.

Stephen O'Hagan (10)
New Row Primary School

There's A Monster!

There's a monster
In my closet,
He's big and tall
And *scary!*

There's a monster
Under my bed,
He's small but
Very hairy.

There's a monster
In the bathroom,
He's always on
The loo.

There's a monster
In the spare room
And he likes his
Privacy too.

There's a monster
In my pocket,
He's tiny
And very cute.

But beware he's
Just as ferocious,
Even though
He is minute!

Cara Bell (10)
New Row Primary School

The Famine's Few Lives

Years ago,
The blight raised its ugly head
And the dark cloud of death
Hovered above our land.

A rank smell
Attacks our nostrils,
. . . We choke . . .
On death in the air.

I have a feeling
That I too shall perish.
A lack of food, stress
But most of all because of the famine.

Órán Donnelly (10)
New Row Primary School

Death And Sickness Have Struck

Sickness has engulfed us,
Children have no clothes,
The hunger is hitting us harder every day,
Disease and illness is everywhere.
The blight has infected the potatoes
And our parents struggle to survive.
'Mum, Dad, come back,' I cry,
'My life is dull without you.'
I'm shedding tears by the bucketful
Until alas I cry no more.

Joeleen Mullan (10)
New Row Primary School

Bad Potatoes

Potatoes rot
While people die.
I feel as if I too am fading away.
My town, my country,
They take their last breath.
What a monstrous smell -
I feel like giving up,
Just falling to the ground so I too will rot away.
It will soon be my time to go
So I'll say my last goodbye . . .
Farewell my once beautiful *Ireland!*

Danielle Beatty (10)
New Row Primary School

What Is Black?

Black is the evil in my nightmares,
Black is the death when you go down those fiery stairs.

Black is the darkness when you close your eyes,
Black is the thunder in stormy skies.

Black is the colour all around you,
Black is nothing like blue.

Black is evil - there's no doubt about it,
But could you imagine living without it?

Ryan O'Kane (11)
New Row Primary School

Life In The Famine

Life in the famine is not any good,
A potato blight flows over our food.
My family tree blows, when is it my turn to go?
As I walk the roads to the workhouse
I can hear screams and cries from the people
Who have passed away and died.
Houses are dirty and smelly, not much room to stay,
I wonder will the future be like this or will it go away.

Nadine Lagan (10)
New Row Primary School

The Sound Collector

(Based on 'The Sound Collector' by Roger McGough)

'A stranger called this morning
Dressed in all black and grey,
Put every sound into a bag
And carried them away'.

The mooing of the cow,
The grunting of the pigs,
The howling of the wind,
The crackling of small twigs.

The chirping of the birds,
The buzzing of busy bees,
The noise of all the animals,
The rustling of leaves.

The snoring of a donkey,
The baaing of soft sheep,
The noise of people talking,
The stamping of their feet.

'A stranger called this morning
He didn't leave his name,
Left us only silence
Life will never be the same'.

Adam Freeman (10)
Portstewart Primary School

The Icicle

The air is quiet,
The surface is smooth,
Its metal shimmers clearly
In the night sky.

It is so very still
Yet vicious,
Sharp and pointed
Is this weapon.

Be careful of it!
Don't let it get you!
Watch out for its deadly blade!
Stay well away!

Shannon Costello (10)
Portstewart Primary School

The Vacuum Cleaner

He moves across the floor,
Slowly but deadly,
Sucking up everything in his path.
His eyes never blink, his face never smiles,
His long snout searching all around.

I've gone upstairs to try and get to sleep.
I hear him scream and hiss,
My mum has him by the neck,
He screams louder and louder,
He's getting closer,
Will I be safe?

William Smyth (10)
Portstewart Primary School

A Tree In Winter

The old man's fingertips
Reach up high
To touch the sky.

His arms arch,
Bare and twisted
The trunk, withered and worn.

He's all alone,
Silent and still,
Fragile and sad.

Dillan Akyol (10)
Portstewart Primary School

The Sea

As roaring as a lion pouncing on its prey.
As quiet as a mouse so it doesn't wake the cat.
As angry as the teacher if you haven't done your homework.
As silent as the wind on a calm day.
As thrashing as a T-rex bashing cars on the ground.
As gentle as the rabbit lovingly being stroked.
As restless as your parents when they didn't get any sleep.
As calm as a bird in a light breeze.

Jenny Mitchell (10)
Portstewart Primary School

A Cow

There once was a fat cow called Mary
Who lived half her life in the dairy.
She ate lots of grass,
Couldn't run very fast,
She fancied a big bull called Jerry.

Tara Nicholl (10)
Portstewart Primary School

Animals

The monkey is a creature,
He's funny as can be,
You'll often see him in the zoo
Dangling from a tree.

The lion is a fierce cat,
The jungle VIP,
With his sharp claws and huge white teeth,
Keep him away from me.

The biggest is the elephant,
He's grey from tail to trunk,
But get in his way when he's on the move,
He'll turn you into junk!

Christopher McNeill (11)
Portstewart Primary School

Holidays

Packing up and leaving
For a holiday,
Suitcase, passport, tickets,
Oh, and spending money!
Getting impatient on the plane,
Excited when we land,
Happy to be there at last,
Sun, sea and sand.
Oh no! Sunlotion,
Takes *ages* to dry.
Ah, yes! Diving with dolphins -
I'd like to give *that* a try!

Andrew Lynch (11)
Portstewart Primary School

Animals

I have a rabbit
With nice fur so long and grey,
Her name is Misty.

She can sometimes bite,
Her breed is a Dwarf Loppy,
With ears so long.

She just drinks water
And eats special rabbit mix,
As well as apples.

She hops on the lawn,
Her hutch has got a chimney
And looks like a house.

Misty is now four,
I got her at eight weeks old,
I'm glad she is mine.

Lois Carson (10)
Portstewart Primary School

Tsunami Disaster

First came an earthquake,
Then a tidal wave came,
People lost everything.

Children lost parents,
Their school and their homes,
Now nowhere to go.

What shall they do?
You can help by giving money,
Please help them!

Natalie Costello (10)
Portstewart Primary School

Blast-Off!

10,
Oh no, I'm shaking.
9,
I wonder where Marrog is?
8,
I want to go home.
7,
I'm going to be rocket sick.
6,
I'm scared of heights.
5,
Where is that stupid seatbelt?
4,
Sweat is trickling down me.
3,
Get me out of here!
2,
Here it goes.
1,
Oh no!
Blast-off!

Patrick Harris (10)
Portstewart Primary School

Nature Cinquain

Nature,
Its raw power
Was demonstrated in
The recent tsunami. It is
Scary.

Richard Nicholl (10)
Portstewart Primary School

The Sound Collector

(Based on 'The Sound Collector' by Roger McGough)

'A stranger called this morning
Dressed all in black and grey,
Put every sound into a bag
And carried them away'.

The sizzling of the cooker,
The banging of the door,
The humming of the kettle,
The squeaking of the floor.

The cutting of the bread knife,
The turning of the lock,
The shouting of my mother
When she sees the clock.

The talking of the TV,
The barking of my dog,
The miaowing of the cat
As it's lost in the fog.

The rustling of my hamster
As he chomps his fill,
The talking of my uncle
Sitting by my friend Bill.

'A stranger called this morning,
He didn't leave his name,
Left us only silence,
Life will never be the same'.

Daniel Burrough (10)
Portstewart Primary School

Valentine Haiku

Cupid is sending
Lots of my kisses to you,
Be my Valentine!

Rachel Millar (11)
Portstewart Primary School

The Sea

As angry as a lion stalking out its prey.
As violent as a bull charging at the crowds.
As powerful as the winds ruining everything in sight.
As wreckful as the tsunami earthquake.
As restless as a baby.

As peaceful as the sun setting.
As quiet as a child sleeping.
As smooth as glass.
As gentle as a puppy.

Kheva Cole (10)
Portstewart Primary School

Palace Guards Cinquain

Guards stand
So tall and slim
Their heads held high and proud
Watching the palace all day long
So brave.

Gavin Darragh (11)
Portstewart Primary School

Adjective Poem

On my way to school one day,
I met a bear,
A brown bear,
A big brown bear,
A big, brown, brainy bear,
A big, brown, brainy, burping bear,
A big, brown, brainy, burping, buccaneering bear,
And it chased me all the way to school.

Hannah Bacon (10)
Portstewart Primary School

The Sound Collector

(Based on 'The Sound Collector' by Roger McGough)

'A stranger called this morning
Dressed all in black and grey,
Put every sound into a bag
And carried them away'.

The blaring of the music,
The barking of the dog,
The popping of the toaster,
The banging of the log.

The purring of a kitten,
The dripping of the tap,
The whistling of the kettle,
The turning of the cap.

The screaming of the baby,
The creaking of the stairs,
The crying of my sister
To see if anyone cares.

The shouting of my mother
To get ready for school,
The loud snoring of my dad.
Crash! I break the stool.

'A stranger called this morning
He didn't leave his name,
Left us only silence
Life will never be the same'.

Leona Howarth (10)
Portstewart Primary School

The Sound Collector

(Based on 'The Sound Collector' by Roger McGough)

'A stranger called this morning
Dressed all in black and grey,
Put every sound into a bag
And carried them away'.

The swishing of the flags,
The thrashing of the rain,
The cheering of the crowd,
The gurgling of the drains.

The bashing of the ball,
The thumping of the feet,
The shouting of the referee
At anyone who cheats.

The hissing of the wind,
The clapping of the players,
The creaking of the stand,
The squeaking of the stairs.

The ticking of the clock
As the tension grows,
The match is finally over,
Referee's whistle blows.

'A stranger called this morning
He didn't leave his name,
Left us only silence
Life will never be the same again'.

Heather Spence (10)
Portstewart Primary School

The Sound Collector

(Based on 'The Sound Collector' by Roger McGough)

'A stranger called this morning
Dressed all in black and grey,
Put every sound into a bag
And carried them away'.

The trotting of the horses
Going down the country lane,
The mooing of the cows
Which is doing in my brain.

The rushing of the leaves,
The buzzing of the bees,
The rumbling of the tractors,
The wind singing through the trees.

The quacking of the ducklings
Bathing in the lake,
The barking of the dogs
While picnickers eat their cake.

The munching of the sheep,
A smile upon its face,
The chirping of the birds
In this perfect place.

'A stranger called this morning
He didn't leave his name,
Left us only silence
Life will never be the same'.

Jane Walker (10)
Portstewart Primary School

The Sea

As angry as a tornado when it spins.
As tame as a dog when it was a pup.
As rough as a boxing match when it begins.
As calm as the rain when it starts.
As big as a tidal wave as it starts to grow.
As smooth as a baby when it is born.
As high as Mount Everest when you reach the top.
As deep as a valley in the Alps.
As vicious as a lion when it looks for its prey.
As gentle as a snowflake as it falls from the sky.

Cristina Corbett (10)
Portstewart Primary School

Valentine's Day Cinquain

Love day
Presents coming
Cards are coming as well
Valentine's Day is coming soon
Hearts meet.

Rebekah Moore (11)
Portstewart Primary School

Hobbies

H ow many hobbies do I have?
O rgan playing,
B odhran (an Irish drum),
B eginning guitar lessons this Friday (*yeah*),
I n the summer I'm getting horse riding lessons,
E very dry day I'm out trampolining,
S ika Gymnastics Club every Thursday.

Rebecca Patterson (10)
Portstewart Primary School

Tornado

See it in the distance,
Twisting up the sea.
See the fish in the
Sky as it passes by.
It comes up on the
Land, people run
And shout,
'There's a
Tornado,
You'd
Better
All
Watch
Out!'

Emma Thompson (10)
Portstewart Primary School

UFO

When I was walking to school,
I saw a UFO.
It was a silver UFO,
It was a clean, silver UFO,
It was a hot, clean, silver UFO,
It was a new, hot, clean, silver UFO,
It was a weird, new, hot, clean, silver UFO,
It was a rude, weird, new, hot, clean, silver UFO.
It zapped me with its laser gun,
It kept following me!
It grabbed me with its arm
And took me to Mars
And left me there.

Corey McDowell (10)
Portstewart Primary School

My Sea Poem

As reckless as a storm destroying everything in its path,
As calm as a baby sleeping very softly,
As angry as a lion eating its prey,
As flat as a flatfish lying on the ocean's bed,
As powerful as a bull charging at a matador's red flag,
As peaceful as the sun setting in the sky,
As violent as boxers fighting in the ring,
As quiet as a star floating all alone in space,
As thrashing as a jockey whipping his horse,
As still as a statue staying in its place.

Jack Taggart (10)
Portstewart Primary School

The Sea

As angry as a lion ready to pounce,
As roaring as a tiger ready for food,
As crashing as the waves across the rock,
As raging as a teacher when she gets cross,
As racing as a motorbike zooming past,
As calm as a baby sleeping soundly,
As peaceful as a quiet afternoon,
As smooth as melted chocolate sitting in my bowl,
As relaxed as a teacher when everyone is quiet,
As tranquil as a hidden lake that nobody knows about.

Maeve Hough (10)
Portstewart Primary School

Swimming Race Cinquain

Chosen
To swim a race,
I do want to win it.
The starter fires the gun, I dive,
I race.

Christopher Coils (11)
Portstewart Primary School

The Sea

Is as angry as a berserk bull rampaging at the matador's red
blazing cape.
Is as quiet as a mouse scaling the floor at midnight.
Is as intense as the mighty Zeus striking down from the heavens,
But as gentle as a fly hovering, exploring, adventuring the night's sky.
As ferocious as a tiger stalking its prey, step by step.
As timid as a newborn baby meeting someone for the first time.
As violent as a hurricane wrecking everything in its path.
As calm as a boat swaying gently in the breeze.
As reckless as an earthquake collapsing everything to rubble.

Daniel Burns (10)
Portstewart Primary School

Football Cinquain

Football
It is my sport
I really love football
I support Liverpool and France
Football.

Jordan Hemphill (11)
Portstewart Primary School

The Sea

As violent as an intense lightning storm.
As brutal as a lion killing a small deer.
As furious as my mum when I don't tidy my room.
As hostile as an angry crowd.
As forceful as the strong wind.
As peaceful as a walk on the deserted beach.
As tranquil as a relaxing holiday in Spain.
As placid as the old sleeping dog.
As still as a statue.
As relaxed as the kitten sleeping in the basket.

Casandra Patton (10)
Portstewart Primary School

Merry Monarch Kennings

1 foot taller
Smaller father
Coffee drinker
Adult thinker
Enemy forgiver
Horse racer
Good dancer
Tennis player
Strong gambler
Monarchy restorer
Great navigator
Money spender
Wig wearer
Army leader
Tree hider
England escaper
Cromwell hater
Popular keeper
Theatre goer
Dog lover
Science liker
Park walker
Plague loather
Fire detester.

Ross Wakefield (11)
Portstewart Primary School

Easter Cinquain

Easter,
Nice chocolate eggs
And an Easter dinner.
Eat all the chocolate I can see,
Easter.

Megan Nelson (11)
Portstewart Primary School

The Writer Of This Poem
(Based on 'The Writer of this Poem' by Roger McGough)

The writer of this poem
Is as small as a baby calf that moos,
As keen as an athlete,
As handsome as Tom Cruise.

As bold as brass,
As light as a feather,
As annoying as a headache,
As strong as the wind in windy weather.

As smooth as a piece of wool,
As quick as a mouse,
As cool as a surfer,
As gruesome as a woodlouse.

As brave as a lion,
As sharp as a dog behind a muzzle,
As tanned as a white shirt,
As tricky as a puzzle.

As smart as Stephen Hawkings,
As cunning as a fox,
As manly as Henry Tudor,
As compact as a box.

*'The writer of this poem
Never ceases to amaze,
He's one in a million billion
(Or so the poem says)'.*

Owen McKinney (11)
Portstewart Primary School

Love Haiku

Love is in the air,
People are buying presents
And giving them too.

Ben Porter (11)
Portstewart Primary School

The Writer Of This Poem

(Based on 'The Writer of this Poem' by Roger McGough)

The writer of this poem
Is as bouncy as a trampoline,
As slow as a snail,
As creative as you've ever seen.

As sweet as sugar,
As happy as a lark,
As mad as a moo,
As exciting as a shark.

As funny as a joker,
As pretty as a flower,
As clever as numbers,
As on time as the hour.

As silly as a goat,
As busy as a bee,
As hot as a fire,
As untanned as you'll ever see.

As daring as a devil,
As loud as a waterfall,
As flexible as rubber,
As cute as a doll!

The writer of this poem
Never ceases to amaze,
She's one in a million billion
(Or so the poem says).

Rachel Wilson (11)
Portstewart Primary School

Merry Monarch Kennings

Moustache wearer
Ugly youngster
Friendly smiler
Knowledge sharer
Coffee drinker
Great dancer
Army leader
Tree hider
England escaper
Cromwell hater
Monarchy restorer
Clothes needer
Money spender
Jewels replacer
Enemy forgiver
Horse rider
Dog lover
Theatre goer
Tennis player
Fire extinguisher
Plague helper
Party starter
Clock winder
Music listener
Maths thinker
Children needer
People carer.

Ashleigh Evans (10)
Portstewart Primary School

Blast-Off!

10,
I'm looking forward to seeing Mars.
9,
I miss my family.
8,
My heart is pumping.
7,
Is it cold or warm or maybe even both?
6,
Do they have beds?
5,
Do they sleep?
4,
Are they small or tall aliens?
3,
I'm probably the only human.
2,
Can they say my name?
1,
Do they have a bathroom?

Blast-off!

Carolanne McGowan (10)
Portstewart Primary School

My Goats Cinquain

My goats
They love their meal
My goats are so lovely
My dad loves them and so do I
My goats.

Marcus Galbraith (11)
Portstewart Primary School

Seasons Haiku Poems

Summer is the best,
It is really hot outside,
Run and shout and play.

Autumn is quite good,
Leaves are yellow, red and brown,
Kicking them around.

Now it's spring, hurrah!
Sometimes sunny, sometimes wet,
Lambs are born today.

Winter is so bad,
It is really cold and wet,
Maybe it will snow.

Aaron Fielding (10)
Portstewart Primary School

Through My Winter Window

Through my winter window
I can see children singing and playing
with a cold breeze and a gentle sneeze
I can see the snow come.

Through my winter window
children playing and dancing
around the Christmas tree
and singing loads more.

Through my winter window
the trees are bare and we are fair
walking away in the snow today
through my winter window.

Shannon O'Kane (10)
St Canice Primary School, Dungiven

Me And My Family

My dad is out building,
My mum is stuck in the house,
My brother is on the PS2
But he's not very nice.

My auntie's out shopping
And never, never stops,
My granny's sitting knitting
And she's knitting a jumper for me.

My baby cousin is
Sitting and messing up my stuff
And is sick all over the lot!

My granda is out farming,
Looking after the sheep and the cows,
And comes back all
Messy and mucky.

What a boring old family!
What a silly lot!
Sometimes I think
I'm the only beautiful one they've got!

Sinéad O'Connor (9)
St Canice Primary School, Dungiven

Stop, Look, Listen

Don't *smoke* it will leave you *broke*
It will make all your friends *choke*.

Don't take that *drug*
Or you'll end up a *thug*.

Don't *drink* it will make you *stink*
Blur your mind and you can't think.

Erin McGuigan (10)
St Canice Primary School, Dungiven

Brid's Christmas List

Dear Santa,
Can I have some of these?

Can I have
A karaoke machine,
A set of DVDs,
Some games for my Game Boy,
A big Christmas dinner
And some tubes of sweets?
That would be nice.

Even though I won't
Get all of them,
I will be happy if I get some.

Thank you Santa,
Yours, Brid.

Brid McCloskey (10)
St Canice Primary School, Dungiven

My Own Christmas List

A bike that goes
A puppy
A kite that blows
A make-up set
A set of dressing up clothes
And dressing up shoes
And a toy dog that doesn't poo
A Barbie
And a Baby Annabell
If I behave very well.

Justine Doherty (9)
St Canice Primary School, Dungiven

Through My Winter Window

Through my winter window
I look out every day
I see snow and snowmen
though I'm not allowed out to play.

In the morning I wake up
and see snowflakes gliding down
lightly flapping, curling round
gently to the ground.

There is ice on the road
and car tracks too,
A robin redbreast flies in the sky
where no other birds flew.

I see children throwing snowballs
and running round our town tree
and others making angel shapes in the snow
and others singing happily.

There is fog on the mountain
in the wilderness but
when I look out my window
I see more than mist
through my winter window.

Conor McCloskey (10)
St Canice Primary School, Dungiven

The Smoke

Over there is a little house
Quiet as a mouse on an empty hive
Or as death
But in the air.

From the chimney pot goes the
Gentle smoke and I know that
The house is alive.
I can see its breath.

Shauna Craig (10)
St Canice Primary School, Dungiven

What Is Man?

Snake hissed and slithered forward
And hid behind the tree,
'Snake, what is it you are up to?'
Called Lemur from a tree.
'I'm looking for Man, so let me be.'
'Do you know what Man is?'
'No, but it sounds small and easy to catch.'
So then a young prankster walked by.
'Excuse me, but could you tell me what Man is?'
'Why yes, man has long ears, a fluffy tail and always jumps,
But you two would be no match,' he giggled.
'We'll see about that.'
So off he went into the jungle.
It was not long before he found a rabbit.
'At last I have caught Man!' shouted the snake.

Eilish McLaughlin (10)
St Canice Primary School, Dungiven

Niall's Christmas List

A PS2 and a few games,
A fast car,
A pair of boots for football matches,
An Ireland home football jersey,
A football book about old soccer
And a few surprises.
I have been a good boy this year
So Santa can you give me a few surprises
And all the things I want this year?
If my presents are enough I will give you
A cup of milk and a bar or two!

Niall O'Kane (9)
St Canice Primary School, Dungiven

Young Writers - Playground Poets Co Londonderry

Through My Winter Window

Through my winter window
I see snowflakes running down.
Santa on the roof bringing the
Toys down the chimney.
Holly hanging down,
Carollers singing merry songs,
Decorating the house with lights,
Car tracks in the snow,
Robin redbreast flying about in the sky.
Christmas trees outside houses, decorated.
Snowflakes flipping, curling, twisting,
Frosty day outside,
Slippery and sludgy.
Playing and laughing.

Michael Brolly (9)
St Canice Primary School, Dungiven

Through My Winter Window

Through my winter window I see a wilderness of white,
Swirling, twisting, twirling snowflakes all about.
The glistening of a crystal lake in ice.
Beautiful patterns upon the window.
As I look out from the window I see a forest in the distance,
Bare trees I see covered in snow, through my winter window.

Through my winter window, happiness is all about.
Snowball fights and birds in flight,
A cheeky little robin who always hops about,
A crafty crow who annoys a doe in the forest park.
Cheerful people all about, through my winter window.

Aoife Hannon (10)
St Canice Primary School, Dungiven

Frankenstein

Frankenstein, the biggest thing in the world
With a bolt through his neck
Like a bolt through iron
And scars on his face
Green head, green hands, green legs
Green body
As green as grass
Bumping up and down with his big green feet
Clothes all raggy
Like Cinderella's clothes
Bolting people with his feet
Burying them under the ground
As every day he does
Look out, look out he might be coming . . .

Lorraine McNicholl (9)
St Canice Primary School, Dungiven

My Crazy Family

My dad is watching football
While my mum is cooking the dinner
My gran is playing bingo but she never
Wins any money.

My brother is playing with cars but he always makes a mess
My sister is trying to get out to her boyfriend
And she has nothing to wear.

What a crazy old family
What a silly old lot
I think I am the only sensible one they've got!

Ciara McLaughlin (9)
St Canice Primary School, Dungiven

My Christmas Thank You Poem

(Based on 'Christmas Thank Yous' by Mick Gower)

Dear Granny,
Thanks for the pyjamas!
Just as long as they're not too comfortable
When I go to sleep.
Conall
xxx.

Dear Uncle,
Thanks for the selection box!
I can't wait to eat it all
But I don't want to be sick.
Conall
xxx.

Dear Roger,
Thanks for the Miniature Heroes
A pity there weren't more
Cadbury Dreams! *Huh!*
Conall
xxx.

Dear Grandma,
Thanks for the PJs!
Now I can't wait to go
To bed!
Conall
xxx.

Conall Mallon (9)
St Canice Primary School, Dungiven

The Mighty White

The mighty white bear will give you a scare,
If you go too near, he'll fill you with fear,
He is big and tough, he will play very rough,
When he sits down for dinner, I would not be enough.

Niall Devine (8)
St Colmcilles Primary School, Claudy

I Wish

I wish . . . I don't know what to wish,
How about I had a thousand pets,
And always won all the bets,
Then I could be a millionaire,
People carrying me about in a golden chair.

I wish, I wish school was more cool,
Maybe even they would turn it into a swimming pool.

I wish, I wish those horrible old teachers, they went away and
When they came back they were turned into creatures.

I wish, I wish, I could take over the world,
And then I'd get my brown hair curled.

I wish, I wish . . . 'Eh, eh hum, Marie-Clare Devine, could you
Please tell me what 145 is divided by eighty-nine?'

I know what to wish for, to learn my times table.

Marie-Clare Devine (9)
St Colmcilles Primary School, Claudy

Winter's Fun

W inter which is cold and fun,
 I cy are the frozen ponds,
N ice presents we all get,
T winkling stars early at night,
E xcitement from everyone around,
R acing snowboards coming down the hill,
S oft snow we all like to play in.

F ussy mothers talking about wrapping up warm,
U nbelievable amount of snow that falls,
N ourishing Christmas dinner which is tasty.

Karen McGlinchey (10)
St Colmcilles Primary School, Claudy

I Wish . . .

I wish I could be a lawyer,
That could go to work every day,
I wish I could be turned into an employer,
Yes, an employer should get a good pay.

I wish I had my own school,
With my money I could buy a sports car,
I wish I could have a private pool,
Maybe my house could turn into a bar.

Caoimhe O'Neill (10)
St Colmcilles Primary School, Claudy

Mammy And Daddy

My mammy and daddy
Are the best parents ever,
I'll never leave them, never ever,
They are always there,
They always care,
And they treat me and
My brothers very fair.

Serena McElhinney (8)
St Colmcilles Primary School, Claudy

Playground Poets

We go out each school day,
At break time and lunchtime to play,
With our friends I like to play,
There are lots of boys and girls running
                    about the playground
Monitors look after the children,
We have so much fun,
We want to stay in the playground and play.

Emmet O'Kane (9)
St Colmcilles Primary School, Claudy

Through My Eyes

Through my eyes,
I can see fields filled with green grass,
Through my eyes,
I can see children running down to class,
Through my eyes,
I can see my brother reading his book,
Through my eyes,
In the morning I can see people hanging their coats on their hooks,
Through my eyes,
I can see cartoons on the telly,
Through my eyes,
I can see Mammy making yummy orange jelly,
Through my eyes,
I can see the clock ticking the minutes by,
Through my eyes,
I can see the grass growing high,
Through my eyes,
I can see my nana knitting a warm woolly hat,
Through my eyes,
I can see my cousin hitting a ball with a bat,
Through my eyes,
I can see everything.

Jodie Carlin (9)
St Colmcilles Primary School, Claudy

Rabbits

My favourite pet is a rabbit,
But I do not like its habit,
It nibbles here, it nibbles there,
I know because I see it everywhere,
It has long ears and a cute little tail,
The one I had didn't like storms or gales.

Michelle McKeever (7)
St Colmcilles Primary School, Claudy

I Wish

I wish I had a limo,
That's very clean and white.
I wish I had the sun,
That's very, very bright.
I wish I had two great big wings,
So I could fly so high,
And then I could see everyone,
From way up in the sky.
I wish I was a footballer,
Who played with Robbie Keane,
And Shay Given and Damien Duff,
On the Irish football team.
I wish I won the Lotto,
So I could buy the zoo -
With elephants, lions
And lots of monkeys too!

Aaron Donaghy (9)
St Colmcilles Primary School, Claudy

The Fierce Crocodile

There once was a fierce crocodile,
Who wasn't even fake,
He lived in a lake,
Where the piranhas always lurked,
He lurks upon his prey,
To make his dinner for the day,
If you go up to that lake,
I advise you not to stay,
Because if you stay up there too long,
I assure you you'll be gone.

Martin Brolly (8)
St Colmcilles Primary School, Claudy

Through My Eyes

Through my eyes I can see,
Playful children running quickly,
Colourful leaves falling happily,
Huge bees flying slowly,
Green grass laying quickly.

Through my eyes I can see,
Beautiful butterflies sitting bravely,
Black spotty dogs barking loudly,
Small spiders crawling somewhere,
Tall aunties shouting often.

Aine McCloskey (10)
St Colmcilles Primary School, Claudy

I Wish, I Wish

I wish, I wish and I wish,
But don't know what to wish for,
Maybe, a dinosaur, kangaroo or swordfish,
Or do I need anything more?
After watching the tsunami on the TV,
My only wish is that the people there,
Will soon be happy as me.

Fionain Smyth (9)
St Colmcilles Primary School, Claudy

I Wish

I wish I could eat lots of sweets,
Without feeling sick,
Or be a great magician,
With lots of special tricks,
A secret spy I'd love to be,
Even Superman would do for me.

Conor Doherty (8)
St Colmcilles Primary School, Claudy

Through My Eyes

Through my eyes is this poem,
I must explain to you alone,
You must know what this poem is about,
When you read it you will want to shout,
So through my eyes I can see,
Two people looking at me,
One's called Mum, the other's called Dad,
They are happy not sad,
My sisters I can also see,
They are an important part of me,
So now you know what's through my eyes,
It makes me happy to be alive.

Colleen Ward (8)
St Colmcilles Primary School, Claudy

I Wish

I wish I had an elephant,
I think I'd call him Jack,
If he was big enough,
I'd put a saddle on his back!
I wish I had an elephant,
Living in my house,
If he was small enough,
I'd use him as a mouse!
I wish I had an elephant
The size of a bat,
If I had a bald head,
I'd use him as a hat!

Cathal O'Reilly (8)
St Colmcilles Primary School, Claudy

I Wish

I wish that I could climb a mountain,
the biggest mountain there is,
I wish that some day I could work in showbiz.
I wish that I could be so tall and
boy, I would have a ball,
I wish that millions of people would gather
around me and shout, 'Yippee.'
I wish I could be in a movie myself,
I could play Santa's little elf.
I wish that I could live in the wild,
even though I'm just a child,
All these things may not come true,
but that is up to me and you.

Loren Ward (8)
St Colmcilles Primary School, Claudy

Through My Eyes

Through my eyes,
I can see birds up in the sky and
A yellow bright sun,
Through my eyes,
I can see dogs chasing cats all day long,
Through my eyes,
I can see children playing all the time.

Through my eyes,
I can see clouds appearing up in the sky,
Through my eyes,
I can see rain pouring down,
Through my eyes,
I can see trees blowing in the breeze.

Shane Brown (9)
St Colmcilles Primary School, Claudy

Through My Eyes

T hrough my eyes I can see the baby who's crying looking for me,
I I orses, horses all around the fields, they are rubbing heads,
R ough seas, bubbly bees swimming, flying all around,
O nly two eyes is all I have so I can't see as much as I thought,
U nbelievable, unbelievable, what have you done? Now I can't see,
　 you can't see.
G reat, great that's all I have to see but it's going to have to be,
H ere we go, here we go to see where we go.

M aybe, maybe may I see me and you together,
Y ou and me, come let's see.

E vil, evil go over to the cable, so I can see you,
Y ou can see me, I can see you so turn around,
E xplore, explore so you can see all,
S leep, sleep go away to sleep.

Maria Kelly (10)
St Colmcilles Primary School, Claudy

Playground Poets

I wish I was tall,
As tall as a house,
With windows like eyes,
As curious as a mouse,
If I was tall,
Then I could play basketball.

If I was tall,
I would be the biggest of them all,
It's terrible being small,
Oh! I wish I was tall.

Cathal O'Neill (9)
St Colmcilles Primary School, Claudy

I Wish

I love Christmas time,
Carol singers make Christmas rhymes,
Every day snow is falling on the ground,
Santa's fairies wave their wands,
Reindeer make no sound,
Santa works really hard,
Children send Christmas cards.

I wish it was Christmas every day,
Christmas will come this way.

Megan Farren (8)
St Colmcilles Primary School, Claudy

In The Playground

On the playground I laugh and play,
Then on Tuesday I play footie,
I play tig with Kieran and Kevin,
And my friend Kevin only looks seven.

Some boys play hopscotch and others watch,
And when it was done, we said we had fun,
The time has come the teacher calls,
Now we have to hand back our footballs.

Ciaran McCloskey (10)
St Colmcilles Primary School, Claudy

The Sneaky Snake

What is that I see?
It's long and slimy,
It is sliding up a tree,
It camouflaged itself in the grass,
'Get me out of this jungle!
Someone help me please!'

Ethan Browne (7)
St Colmcilles Primary School, Claudy

Playground Poets

P is for playground, where I have fun with my friends,
L is for laughing when Jordan tells us a joke,
A is for autumn when we jump in a pile of leaves,
Y is for yelling when we're laughing and playing,
G is for games that we play every break,
R is for running in our sports day races,
O is for outside where we play two times a day,
U is for understanding all of the rules of our games,
N is for noises and there's lots in the playground,
D is for dodgeball, my favourite game.

Jordan Hone (9)
St Colmcilles Primary School, Claudy

My Pancake Poem

Little, little pancake,
Tossing all about,
Up in the air,
And all around.
Put it in the pan,
Turn it all around,
Make sure it's cooked,
So don't make a sound.

Emma McCloskey (8)
St Colmcilles Primary School, Claudy

Dog

I have a dog named Sofie,
She is brown, short, furry and friendly,
When she's on her lead, she likes to run and walk,
At home she likes to pounce,
Her favourite food is bones,
In a year, she'll be one stone,
And that's my poem about my puppy dog.

Aileen Burke (8)
St Colmcilles Primary School, Claudy

The Dog

Once upon a time,
There was a dog who was called Gismo,
He lived in Tyrone,
He was a sheepdog,
He was my nana's,
She owned Gismo the dog,
He ran through the fields,
I got out of the car,
And Gismo jumped up on me.

Naomi Martin (7)
St Colmcilles Primary School, Claudy

Monkeys

Monkeys are brown,
They can climb, they can walk,
But you know they can't talk,
They live in the jungle,
With the lions,
They climb up trees and
Swing from tree to tree,
They play with the other monkeys,
In the jungle.

Sean Curran (8)
St Colmcilles Primary School, Claudy

My Dog

My dog is cute and white,
In the sun he looks very bright,
When children go by, he gives them a fright,
Oh my dog is such a beautiful sight!

My dog is funny and white,
When we go for a walk he pulls me along,
Oh how I wish my dog could talk.

Paidi Donaghy (7)
St Colmcilles Primary School, Claudy

Pet Puppies

Puppies and kittens hop, pounce and run,
Playing all day in the hot, hot sun,
Then one day my friend came round,
For there were loads and loads of pups all over the ground,
There was Vince, Sam, Stella, Polly and Max,
John, Mike, Jo, Wendy and Pax.

Pax and Max were twins,
We had a race and Pax wins,
All the dogs went crazy,
Especially Daisy,
Daisy has a crush on Pax,
But poor little Max.

Then one day Una had a puppy,
We called her Yuppy,
Yuppy was very naughty fighting with another puppy,
Polly had a bleeding paw,
The blood went all over the kitchen floor,
When I got home I nearly fainted,
The floor in the kitchen looked like it was painted,
Then I noticed that Polly was beside Yuppy and
                        Polly's paw was bleeding
'Yuuupppy,' I shouted. 'You bad puppy,'
I sent Yuppy to the Rascal Basket,
Yuppy would not go to the puppy picnic,
When we left for the picnic,
Yuppy got very sick,
When the dogs and I got home,
We saw Yuppy could not roam,
She fainted,
When she woke up,
She noticed she was now called Yup.

Emily Clayton (7)
St Colmcilles Primary School, Claudy

Man United

M an United, glory, glory,
A ble to beat any team,
N asty Kezman, class Saha.

U nited, best team ever,
N istelrooy forward for United,
I ncredible United,
T all Saha, small Rooney,
E very team cannot beat United,
D avid Beckham used to play for United.

Kevin Ward (10)
St Colmcilles Primary School, Claudy

Zoe

My cousin Zoe is a very special girl,
Zoe is 3 years old and she is not very bold,
She is learning to talk and is ready to walk,
Zoe makes funny faces and she pulls out my laces,
Zoe loves to pull my hair and I say, 'That's not fair.'
I love my cousin Zoe,
I'm as happy as can be when she
Comes to play with me.

Erin O'Kane (8)
St Colmcilles Primary School, Claudy

My Poem Of My Bird

I have a little bird and Joey is his name,
Every time I let him, he plays all sorts of games,
He whistles and he sings like the birds in spring,
When I come home from school, I put him in his bath,
Where it's nice and cool,
When he is fast asleep, he does not make a cheep.

Shauna McCloskey (8)
St Colmcilles Primary School, Claudy

Patch The Sheepdog

Patch is my brother's dog,
He is black and white and fluffy,
He runs, jumps, digs and plays ball,
He comes to Chris when he hears him call,
Some days Patch will run after sheep,
Other days he likes to sleep,
Most of all he's a really good friend,
He barks at strangers and that's the end.

Shaune Gormley (8)
St Colmcilles Primary School, Claudy

My Favourite Person

MY favourite person is my dad,
He cheers me up when I am sad,
He stops fights between me and my mummy,
He gives me medicine when I have a sore tummy,
He takes me to the swimming pool,
I think my dad is really cool,
He is a great lad,
That's why my favourite person is my dad.

Ellen Hendron (8)
St Colmcilles Primary School, Claudy

Kangaroos

Kangaroos, kangaroos they live in the west,
Kangaroos, kangaroos they are the best,
Kangaroos, kangaroos they leap and they jump,
Kangaroos, kangaroos they change every month,
Kangaroos, kangaroos they are very furry,
Kangaroos, kangaroos they love McFlurrys.

Fintan Gormley (7)
St Colmcilles Primary School, Claudy

Springtime

I love the spring,
When the birds do sing,
And the lambs skip across the fields,
Twigs are collected for the nest,
So the birds can have their rest,
The baby chicks will soon be here,
A few weeks, they'll disappear,
They'll fly up to the sky,
And don't look back or say goodbye.

Laura Duffy (8)
St Colmcilles Primary School, Claudy

I Wish

I wish I was model who could model on the stage,
I wish I was a gymnast who could do flips all day.

I wish I was an actress who could act in the street,
I wish I could get a dog, it would be better than a frog.

I wish I could go to see Liverpool play,
I wish I had more money to pay.

I wish I didn't have to say goodbye,
I wish to see you next time.

Megan Harkin (9)
St Colmcilles Primary School, Claudy

In The Playground

In the playground I can see kids,
Big kids, small kids, thin kids, fat kids, funny kids.

In the playground I can see birds,
Big birds, small birds, funny birds, nice birds.

In the playground I can see trees,
Tall trees, small trees, brown trees, green trees.

Connor Bradley (8)
St Colmcilles Primary School, Claudy

My Spurs Heroes

I wish I could play football with Robbie Keane,
Everyone knows he's a dominating machine,
All he ever does is score,
And all the crowd jump and roar.

I wish Jermaine Defoe and me were a striking pair,
For all the defenders we'd give them a scare,
Me and Jermaine we'd be good friends,
And our scoring record would never end.

Ledley King, the king of the defence,
And for all the strikers, he's a fence,
Ledley is a good defender,
And if he was a striker he would kick ball benders.

Niall Logue (9)
St Colmcilles Primary School, Claudy

My Best Friends

Off to school
Friends are waiting at the front gate,
Must hurry or I will be late,
Things won't be cool!

At school two friends are there,
One gets the bus,
Bell rang time to go in,
Back to work must rush.

Spelling test is over,
School is over too,
Mobile rings, Cara is on it,
Friday night off to the cinema.

My friends are so cool!

Niamh Quigg (9)
St John's Primary School, Swatragh

Me, Me I'm Misunderstood

Me, me
I'm misunderstood
My mum thinks I'm rude, my dad thinks I'm crude
And teachers, oh you don't want to know what they think of me.
It's not my fault I'm sloppy and positively dopey in class
But it's only on the skin, on the inside I'm smart
I can answer a question in a flash
But I'd rather save my energy for video games and football!
So I guess they're a bit right
But still me, me I'm misunderstood!

Clodagh McKeefry (10)
St John's Primary School, Swatragh

Snowman

A snowman in my garden,
Looks very cold,
Hat on its head,
Snow on its toes,
Snowflakes all around it,
I wonder if it knows!

Lauren Elliott (7)
St John's Primary School, Swatragh

Strong Winds

The wind blew hard,
Trees fell over,
Hats and scarves blew too!
You have to play inside,
It's fun too!
Listening to the noises and watching out the window,
Staying inside,
Until the wind stops.

Aine O'Kane (7)
St John's Primary School, Swatragh

Water

Water
Water, water everywhere
Hot, cold, nothing else
Always wet
Never dry.

Water, water
In the air
Dripping, dripping down
Jumping in the water
Splashing everywhere.

Kate McKeefry (7)
St John's Primary School, Swatragh

Snowman

Snowman in my garden,
Family inside,
Keeping warm,
Looking outside,
At the snowman,
Snowman feels sad,
Family is warm,
Cosy and dry too!
Come outside and have fun with me!

Catherine McCloy (7)
St John's Primary School, Swatragh

Snowman

Looks cold,
Has scarf, hat too,
Snowman all alone,
All inside, warm by the fire,
In the dark,
In bed snug and warm!

Cathy Harkin (7)
St John's Primary School, Swatragh

Yes!

Crying for my test results,
Listening for the clatter of the letterbox,
Waiting for envelope to slap the ground,
Here he comes, strolling up the driveway,
Gazing at the envelope as it gets pushed through the flap,
It slaps the ground,
Shaking as I pick it up,
My heart started pounding,
My blood was bubbling, my face went red,
Slit open its neck, *yes.*

John Quigg (11)
St John's Primary School, Swatragh

Bears Everywhere

Bears are everywhere
I don't know why.
Well, not everywhere,
Not in my village anyhow.
Would be funny seeing a grizzly
Walking down the streets here
Hunting for his lunch!

Eimear Browne (7)
St John's Primary School, Swatragh

Jack Frost

Ice on his nose,
He's nipping my toes,
He's nipping my hands,
At my window,
I see Jack Frost,
Icicles hanging on my window sill,
He makes me cold, shining outside,
Warm inside, that's where I'll stay.

Patrick Turner (7)
St John's Primary School, Swatragh

Snowman

Snowman has a carrot for a nose,
He wears buttons,
And has a scarf to keep warm,
Branches for his arms,
Body made of snow,
It's freezing outside,
And snowing, snowing,
But he doesn't mind,
Snow all around the snowman.

Sean Dillon (7)
St John's Primary School, Swatragh

Rain

At night it rains,
And in the daytime it rains,
Lots of times it rains,
Rain, rain, rain!
So I would need to get
My umbrella,
I don't want to get wet!

Peadar Coyle (7)
St John's Primary School, Swatragh

Snowflakes

Snowflakes,
Landing on my palm,
Stays a little while,
Then it melts,
Another one lands on my palm,
Shining on my palm,
Then blew away.

John McCormack (7)
St John's Primary School, Swatragh

In The Morning

Laying in bed,
I scratch my head.

Mum gives a shout
'Come on, everybody out.'

There's noise all around,
Pop goes the toast.

Oh there's a van,
It's the postman.

On my way to school,
I see a gang that's cool.

Talking to their friends,
While walking around the bend.

Bronagh McKeefry (10)
St John's Primary School, Swatragh

In Five Minutes I Can

I can ride a horse in five minutes,
I can do 14 handstands in five minutes,
I can score five goals in penalty kicks in five minutes,
I can tidy my room in five minutes,
I can draw a picture in five minutes,
In five minutes I can write a story,
In five minutes I can read a book,
I can do PE,
I can play the flute and the tin whistle in five minutes,
In five minutes I can swim a length.

Eimear Cassidy (7)
St John's Primary School, Swatragh

Fantastic Green

Green is the colour of leaves
Which fall off the trees in the autumn,
Green is the colour of the grass,
Which grows in the spring,
Green is the colour of a crocodile,
Which is scaly and fierce.

Green is the colour of a cactus,
Which is spiky and dangerous,
Green is the colour of an apple,
Which is sweet and juicy,
Green is the colour of my eyes,
Which are bright and colourful,
Green is my favourite colour.

Stephen Coyle (10)
St John's Primary School, Swatragh

The Bright Colour Red

Red, red the bright colour red,
Bright, bright shiny red,
And when I go to bed all I
Can think of is the colour red.

Red is like the colour of an apple,
Sour, tasty and juicy,
When I eat a strawberry it makes
Me scrunch my eyes because they are
So bitter but so tasty.

Claire McGuigan (10)
St John's Primary School, Swatragh

Here Comes The Robot

Here comes the robot,
Bizz, bizz, crunch,
He's looking in the fridge,
Looking for his lunch.

Here comes the robot,
Bizz, bizz, creak,
He's opening the door,
Walking down the street.

Here comes the robot,
Bizz, bizz, thump,
He's running round the room,
Watch out! *Bump, bump!*

Victoria Lagan (7)
St John's Primary School, Swatragh

My Mum

My mum
Is kind to me,
Has brown hair,
Works in Maghera,
Tucks me in at night,
Plays games with me,
Likes to go on walks,
Likes to go out on bike rides,
Makes nice dinners for me,
Likes to watch TV with me,
Likes to read books,
Likes to play on the trampoline with me.

Aimee McQuillan (8)
St John's Primary School, Swatragh

Waiting For Results

Waiting, waiting and more waiting
Oh what mark will I get?
I am so, so, so excited
What school will I go to?
So many questions,
I want the answers!
Now!
What will my friends get?
I wonder
The morning has come
I open the envelope
I got a . . . B2, I passed
Everything went silent
Then . . . 'Yippee!'

Eiméar O'Kane (10)
St John's Primary School, Swatragh

My Mammy

My mammy makes the dinner,
My mammy brings me to school,
My mammy washes the dishes,
My mammy does the bedrooms,
My mammy makes the lunch,
My mammy makes cornflake buns,
She reads me a book,
She walks with me and my family,
She says goodnight to me,
My mammy is special to me because
She loves me a lot.

Eileen Quigg (8)
St John's Primary School, Swatragh

Mystic Yellow

Yellow is the colour of the big bright sun,
Shining in the sky,
Yellow is the colour of the buzzing bumblebees,
Flying way up high.

Yellow is the colour of the bright buttercups,
Growing in the grass,
Yellow is the colour of the fuzzy baby ducks,
Quacking as they pass.

Yellow is the colour of a jumper,
Like a big bright beam,
Yellow is the colour
Of banana ice cream.

Yellow is the colour of the daffodils in spring,
Shaped a bit like a bell,
Yellow is the colour of the cute baby chicks,
They're so cuddly, can't you tell?

Yellow is the tasty banana,
Moon-shaped and ripe,
Yellow is the bittersweet lemon,
But really that's not my type.

Yellow is the colour of the colouring-in pencil,
On paper it's a beautiful thing,
Yellow is the colour of the ink in the pen,
Bright and glittering.

Sara Dillon (10)
St John's Primary School, Swatragh

September

Leaves turning different colours and falling off the trees.
Starting back to school, we rake the leaves to jump in,
After, leaves still flying wild, turning around and around,
Turning from green to gold, brown and red.

Bronagh McKeown (9)
St John's Primary School, Swatragh

Fascinating Red

Red is a fascinating colour,
It reminds me of hot burning fire,
It warms me up on a cold winter's night.

Red is like a sunset,
Beautiful and so bright,
It gives you a warm feeling.

Red is like a rose,
Pretty with a lovely scent,
They're gorgeous in the summertime.

Red is like a strawberry,
Sweet, tasty and juicy.

Red is like Man U,
The roars when they score.

Rachel Donnelly (10)
St John's Primary School, Swatragh

July

Summer holidays finally come,
Everyone out having fun,
Pack your bags and come to Spain,
Here comes Spain,
So get on a plane,
If you stay at home,
Don't stay alone,
The summer sun is full of fun,
So get out and have some fun!

Aimee Harkin (9)
St John's Primary School, Swatragh

August

It's near the end of our holiday,
We'll soon be back to school,
It is so, so cool,
Today is very sunny,
We are going to the beach,
I cannot wait to get there,
No teachers here to teach,
We are going swimming,
Swimming out to sea,
We are going swimming,
Just my friend and me.

Anna Shiels (9)
St John's Primary School, Swatragh

November

The 5th of November is Guy Fawkes' night,
As the bonfires give out light,
November is the month before Christmas,
There isn't much snow today,
But when it becomes December, the snow will be OK.

Ryan Crawford (9)
St John's Primary School, Swatragh

May

May is Mary the mother of Jesus' month,
A May alter is waiting, so let's make it today,
We need white cloth and flowers and a statue as well,
May is the time to say goodbye to your lambs,
Because they're too big to keep anymore.

Rebecca McKeefry (9)
St John's Primary School, Swatragh

When I'm Older . . .

When I'm older . . .
I'll go to the Elk
I'll put on make-up
I'll wear fancy clothes and be the belle of the ball.

When I'm older . . .
I'll go in a sulk because I don't get my own way
I'll be grumpy every day
I'll stamp my feet and scream if someone annoys me.

When I'm older . . .
I'll stay in my room all the time
I'll shout at anyone who comes in
I'll only come out when I absolutely need to.

But for now I'll enjoy being me
Because the time will come. Soon.

Aisling McMullan (11)
St John's Primary School, Swatragh

May

We put up an altar,
We pick bluebells for it is Our Lady's month,
She has a son, Jesus Christ,
May is in spring,
In May we take walks to the river,
We go to the forest,
To pick bluebells,
Winter stopped, spring ends,
In May we help Grandad.

Phillip Convery (8)
St John's Primary School, Swatragh

When The Dragon Came To Our School

He was flying into the school playground
Came into our classroom
Played football at break time
Helped our team beat the others
Watched us doing our work
Skipped with the girls at lunchtime
We had PE
Dragon did PE too
Liked our history class
Did he learn much?

Ciaran Lagan (8)
St John's Primary School, Swatragh

February

February is very, very cold,
A nice big mug of hot chocolate to hold,
We are back at school now,
I wonder how my friends have got on, how?
A snowman melting in the weak sun,
And children having lots of fun,
Snowdrops are starting to appear,
Over there! Over here!

Mark Mellon (9)
St John's Primary School, Swatragh

My Mum

My mum is good to me
My mum is good to me because she bakes me buns
My mum reads me a story at night
My mum takes me to Grandad and Granny's
My mum makes the dinner
She takes me to school
She takes me to Barry's.

John Walsh (7)
St John's Primary School, Swatragh

Waiting

I am so bored my plane has been delayed for five hours
I am so bored, I am going to Spain.
And I have read my book four times already
I am so bored, I can't say how bored I am
I am half asleep and half awake,
But I am so bored all I have done is eaten and drank.
Four hours to go, I am sitting watching my watch
And it just goes *tick-tock, tick-tock*.
Three hours to go now and all I can see are two little twins
All I can hear is music.
Two hours to go now, I'll play some cards and sip some Coke.
One hour to go now,
But I am still bored.
It's four o'clock now, but we will not be getting on till half-five,
I'll do some extra work for my big school
It has just ticked half-five, we are starting to board now.
Sitting in the plane and the captain said,
'Please fasten seat belts, fasten seat belts.'
And off we go.

Sarah Quigg (11)
St John's Primary School, Swatragh

October

In October it is quite cold,
Lots of fireworks being sold,
The clock goes back one hour in October,
Dressing up time will soon be over,
Sometimes we go to firework displays,
Meet our friends and shout hip hip hooray,
During October we dress up at night,
Go round houses, give them a fright,
Sometimes we go trick or treating,
Get some sweets that are nice for eating.

Cathal Quinn (8)
St John's Primary School, Swatragh

My Friends

My friends are really kind to me,
Sometimes I get them, over to my house, to play,
But not every day,
I always wish they could stay.

They always keep me going,
It would be better if we could
Go outside when it is snowing,
Although, it's summer.

We have good fun together,
I hope we will be friends forever,
We won't ever fight, never,
And that's my friends.

Emma McPeake (10)
St John's Primary School, Swatragh

Driving Down The Road

When I'm driving down the road,
I hear a croaking toad
The cars are going past,
Very, very fast
I like a lot of noise,
But I really hate boys
I say my prayers
As I rush down the stairs
When I go to school
I try to be cool
I say bye to Dad
Before he gets mad.

Aoife Coyle (9)
St John's Primary School, Swatragh

I Can't Wait

I can't wait until I'm a teen
Dancing at the disco, what a scene.

I can't wait until I wear a belly top
Then I'll buy a mini skirt in a really dear shop.

I can't wait until I get a car
I'll drive faster and faster and really far.

I can't wait until I have to work
Lots of money and a great big smirk.

I can't wait until I go away on my own
Spain, France and maybe even Rome.

But I guess I'll have to wait
For my time to come
To growing up and having lots of fun.

Rebecca Lagan (10)
St John's Primary School, Swatragh

Friends

F riends are people who care for you every day.

R unning, jumping and skipping when we play.

I n the morning, in the evening, we will be with each
   other day and night.

E ven when we are apart,
   all my friends will be in my heart.

N ever a day that goes by that we make each other cry.

D on't like it when we fight.

S o that's why we're best friends every day.

Niamh McEldowney (10)
St John's Primary School, Swatragh

Waiting For My Results

Sitting by the window,
Waiting for the Royal Mail,
It's a wet and windy day,
Oh when will it come?

Sitting by the window,
Wondering what to do,
Hold on, I see that bright red van.

Sitting by the window,
Here comes the Royal Mail,
I have a woozy
Feeling in my tummy,
I'm feeling hot and sweaty.

Sitting by the window,
In comes the envelope,
I cut its throat open,
Out comes the tongue,
What is the future for me?

Danielle McKeefry (10)
St John's Primary School, Swatragh

He's A Dream Pet, He's My Pet

My pet, my pet is a wonderful pet, I think you might agree!
He can climb on a wall, a tree and clothes, only if you are watching TV.
He has wonderful skin, golden-yellow, dark and dark black,
White as a cloud, orange as an orange, he climbs the bark of trees.
Some people think he is a dinosaur or a small crocodile
But he does not bite as far as I know.
He is a dream pet, a little pet, he is a pet that would cheer you up
When you are sad, he's a pet that loves to climb.
Guess what he is, he is a sad little baby lizard gecko.

Thomas O'Hagan (11)
St John's Primary School, Swatragh

Waiting

Waiting for the results
Sitting on the stairs
Mum's watching TV
Acting like she doesn't care.

Still waiting on the stairs
Waiting for the big white van
Can I see it coming round the corner?
Oh yes, yes I can!

I've been waiting for five seconds
But it seems like five years
I have finally got the envelope
Will I be happy or sobbing tears?

Catherine McCloskey (11)
St John's Primary School, Swatragh

Shining Red

Red is for apples
Which are round and clean.
Red is for a tractor
Which is noisy and ear-splitting.
Red is for a strawberry
Which is juicy and bright.
Red is for my book
Which is colourful and short.
Red is for string
Which is long and furry.
Red is for a chair
Which is peaceful and comfortable.

John Joe Quigg (10)
St John's Primary School, Swatragh

November

November brings the bare trees,
The winter breeze,
The bonfires are burning and sparkling,
November, November brings the winter breeze,
Get out your hats and scarves,
For it is getting cold,
We say our prayers on All Saint's Day,
Light the first candle on the wreath,
To show Christmas is coming near.

Ciara Browne (9)
St John's Primary School, Swatragh

April

April is the middle month of spring,
The sun is starting to come out and
The daffodils are growing,
The baby lambs are growing too,
Easter is on its way,
April has 30 days and is the fourth month of the year,
We play a trick on April Fools Day.

Sean Quinn (9)
St John's Primary School, Swatragh

January

Sometimes in January it snows,
The gentle stream flows,
Only the children enjoy the snow,
Pretty children are cold with the blow,
It is cold in winter, we don't know why,
The only thing we would wish for is to fly,
All we want is more ice,
Because we think it is nice.

Patrick Lagan (9)
St John's Primary School, Swatragh

May

Summer is coming on its way,
It's the end of spring, for now it is May,
It is May, the month of Mary,
Now spring showers are beginning to get weary,
Flowers growing in the grass,
The air is nice here, definitely no gas,
Two more months and we're off school,
Hooray! Hooray! This is so cool!

Kathryn Mullan (9)
St John's Primary School, Swatragh

Love

Love tastes like candyfloss
It sounds like a caterpillar moving
It looks like trees rustling
It smells like baby cream
It feels like a big bunch of grapes
Its colour is red.

Cathair Glass (8)
St Mary's Primary School, Maghera

Hate

Hate is black like hair,
It looks like a bad witch,
It sounds like someone scraping on the blackboard,
It smells like onions,
It tastes like Brussel sprouts,
It feels like a spider.

Enda Gallagher (9)
St Mary's Primary School, Maghera

My Teacher

My teacher is a bright rose
She is a BMW
And is a delicious red apple
She is a bright summer afternoon
She is a blonde leopard
She is a cheerful pink
She is a casual dresser
And is a Harry Potter book.

Luke Fullerton
St Mary's Primary School, Maghera

Happiness

It sounds like a dozen harps
It looks like some people having a great laugh
Happiness is like a cloud of colour
It tastes like a tasty Mars bar
It smells like a colourful flower
It feels like a silky spider's web.

Jude Doherty (8)
St Mary's Primary School, Maghera

Hate

Hate feels like a rock falling on you
Hate is black like the night
Hate looks like devils
Hate tastes like beer
Hate smells like smelly gas
Hate sounds like thunder.

Shannon Burke (9)
St Mary's Primary School, Maghera

Love

It feels like sinking into a bath
with lots of hot water.
It looks like the light blue in the sky.
It tastes like a chocolate bar.
It smells like a very nice perfume.
It looks like a fluffy dog running towards you.
It feels like a soft sponge.

Conor Convery (9)
St Mary's Primary School, Maghera

Joy

Joy is a bag of sweets
Joy is a game of football
Joy is looking at nature
Joy is for walking on the beach
Joy is leaving school happy
Joy is a wonderful thing
Joy is playing with my friends
Joy is playing my PlayStation 2.

Gavin Toner (9)
St Mary's Primary School, Maghera

Happiness

Happiness smells like a blooming flower,
Happiness sounds like soft music
Happiness looks like the sunset
Happiness tastes like the sweetest thing you could imagine
Happiness is the colour of a rainbow
Happiness feels like paradise.

Ciaran McCloy (9)
St Mary's Primary School, Maghera

My Dog

We got her as a Christmas present,
When she rifts, it ain't so pleasant,
She's fun to joke with and play about,
She stares at the water and scares the trout.

Meg is dopey all round,
She'll never be a hunting hound,
Meg will never be a silent creeper,
She is more of a loud, snoring sleeper.

Meg loves to play with a ball,
When she bursts it, she thinks herself tall,
She loves to run about on the grass,
When she gets the ball, she will not pass.

I remember once Meg banged her head off a bin,
I could've swore her head was a tin,
She'll be scared of the hose any day,
If you go near it, she'll run away.

She is scared of the hose, but stands out in the rain,
If you hit her, she'll feel no pain,
Although she's dumb, not as smart as a frog,
She will always be my dog.

Maeve Morren (11)
St Mary's Primary School, Maghera

Really Wild Pumas

Pumas are smart
They kill to eat
Their strong legs are to chase
And jump and catch
Strong bones are to climb trees.

Ciaran O'Hagan (9)
St Mary's Primary School, Maghera

Magic

There is magic everywhere - you can see it,
It's the blue up in the sky,
And the green in the grass.
Or the smell of Mummy's cooking
And the twinkle in an eye.
Magic is all around us!
Give it to a person who is very, very sad
And make them very glad.
Or forgive someone who has been very, very bad.
So let us have some magic,
And then we can party!
It's amazing how a smile
Can last a long, long while.
All you need is magic!

Bronagh McGuckin (8)
St Mary's Primary School, Maghera

Joy

Joy is a bag of sweets
Joy is watching Man Utd play
Joy is books
Joy is writing
Joy is the TV
Joy is Old Trafford
Joy is a Toyota
Joy is my friend Fred
Joy is Alex Ferguson
Joy is my PlayStation 2
Joy is Wayne Rooney.

Shane Turner (8)
St Mary's Primary School, Maghera

My Brother

He smells
He acts like a baby
He gets all the attention
He bites
He fights
He kicks
He roars
He rolls in the mud.
He gets me into trouble
He takes his dog everywhere.
He eats with his mouth open
He burps aloud at dinner time.
He blames everything on me
He breaks Mum's china
He says rude words.
When I get money I have to spend it on *him*
It's hard being an older sister.

Niamh McFalone (9)
St Mary's Primary School, Maghera

A Winter's Day

As I go out the door I see a lot of flustered children playing
Snowballs in the snow as the white gentle snowflakes drift
Upon all.

As I go out the door I hear a lot of joyful shouts
And hard hailstones on my coat.

As I go out the door I feel the soft, tickling snowflakes
Float softly upon my cheeks.

As I step back indoors I smell the sweet smell of cherries
And bubbling hot soup wafting up my nose
As I sit down I taste boiling hot cocoa
And golden, crispy, savoury turkey.

Una Dowdall (11)
St Mary's Primary School, Maghera

Winter Times

The trees stand naked
The hot fire brings red
Rosy-red cheeks
I can hear leaves crunch as I walk
Cars crawling up the hill
I can hear children playing in the snow
I can feel my hands raw and cold
My toes blistering red and numb
Glistening white snowflakes drop down on me
I can smell crispy, golden turkey
Bubbling hot stew
I can taste sizzling hot soup
Lovely, hot, burning potatoes.

Meghan Irwin (10)
St Mary's Primary School, Maghera

Winter Endings

Silvery icicles are glistening in the damp sunlight
I spot a little robin redbreast fluttering to a tree
The shimmering little snowflakes fall
Crisp, golden turkey for a Christmas dinner
I slurp sizzling soup
I finish it off with a nice hot chocolate
I hear a dove twitter in a tree
I hear biting winds filter in the air
I hear blazing fires crackle in the homes
I feel nippy wind as cold as ice
I touch dancing snowflakes falling in the air
Warm winter woollies heat me up
As winter ends the flowers blossom and it is spring again.

James Grant (10)
St Mary's Primary School, Maghera

My Sister

Bites,
Fights,
Screams at nights,
Writes on walls,
Plays with dolls,
Fills her nappy,
Then she's happy,
Eats sweets,
Gives me the creeps,
Hogs the TV.
Would anyone like to buy her from me?

Karl Quinn (9)
St Mary's Primary School, Maghera

My Autumn Haiku Poem

Colourful red leaves
Fluttering, twirling orange leaves
Crunchy yellow leaves.

Aine Craig (11)
St Mary's Primary School, Maghera

My Diamond Poem

Ireland
Tough times
Fever, sickness, disease
Britain, Australia, Canada, America
Potato blight and hungry people
Coffin ships at sea
Starving men working
Black 47
Famine.

Thomas McErlean (11)
St Mary's Primary School, Maghera

My Friend

Our friend is ginger.
He is a revving Ford Focus
He is a mad monkey
And a miserable winter.
He is Basil Brush
He is a hot summery day
He is a football *mad* book
He is a picked onion and cheese sandwich.

Aidan McCoy (10)
St Mary's Primary School, Maghera

A Haiku Poem About Witches

Screeching, ugly, fat
Broomstick flying up so high
Magic green cat purrs.

Joanne Eppleston (11)
St Mary's Primary School, Maghera

Love

Love is yellow like a nice little chick,
It feels like a soft teddy,
It smells lonely and comfortable,
It sounds like softness floating like the wind.

Niamh Ledgewood (8)
St Mary's Primary School, Maghera

Anger

Anger is dark and dull like black or grey.
It tastes like raw cabbage.
It smells like chlorine.
It looks like a filthy pigsty.
It sounds like one hundred trains coming at you.
It feels like a rock.

Shauna McCloskey (9)
St Mary's Primary School, Maghera

Happiness

Happiness looks like big happy smiles.
It tastes like hot pancakes with sugar and rich syrup.
It feels like runny butter melting on toast.
It feels like a smooth, cuddly teddy bear.
Happiness is like a warm rose.
It sounds like birds singing in the warm air.

Shea Leyden (9)
St Mary's Primary School, Maghera

Hate

Hate smells like twelve dead rats.
Hate sounds like a dragon.
Hate tastes like alcohol.
Hate is the colour of a dark night.
Hate feels like someone screaming in your ears.
Hate looks like sour milk.

Aiden McGrath (9)
St Mary's Primary School, Maghera

My Diamond Poem

Ireland.
Sickness develops.
Poor frightened people.
Poverty, fever and blight.
Black 47 was very painful.
Britain, Australia, Canada, America
Despair, worried families.
Tough times.
Typhus.

Nuala Convery (11)
St Mary's Primary School, Maghera

Anger

Anger is as dark as an underwater cave,
It is as fierce as a lion,
It is as cranky as your brother waking you up,
It looks like mouldy oranges,
It smells like slurry in a field,
It sounds like a building collapsing to the ground.

Kim McFalone (8)
St Mary's Primary School, Maghera

Anger

Anger is as red as blood,
It looks like a cross ape,
It sounds like a gorilla squeezing your hand,
It tastes like rotten apples,
It smells like monkeys.

Sean McIlvenny (9)
St Mary's Primary School, Maghera

Hate

Hate is the colour black,
Hate smells like rotten cheese,
It looks like a dark force,
Hate feels like lightning striking you,
It sounds like a siren,
Hate tastes like rotten bread.

Shea Gribbon (9)
St Mary's Primary School, Maghera

Happiness

Happiness is yellow like bees.
It feels like a silky spider's web.
It sounds like a party.
It looks like having a great laugh.
It tastes like a hot dog.

Piaras Flanagan (8)
St Mary's Primary School, Maghera

Love

It smells like daffodils,
It feels like a soft teddy,
It tastes like a chocolate heart,
It sounds like two birds singing in the sky,
It looks like a heart in the air,
Love is red like a heart.

Charlotte Burke (8)
St Mary's Primary School, Maghera

Love

The colour of love is red.
Love feels like a fluffy pillow
Love smells like lots of flowers
Love tastes like candyfloss
Love looks like a big heart
Love sounds like birds singing.

Kerry Johnson (9)
St Mary's Primary School, Maghera

Happiness

Happiness is a pink fluffy cushion
Happiness sounds like nice and smooth music
Happiness tastes like a strawberry milkshake
Happiness smells like perfume in the air
Happiness feels gentle and sweet
Happiness looks like a pink star in the sky.

Sarah Grant (9)
St Mary's Primary School, Maghera

Sadness

Sadness is like a blue line
It smells like a cow
It looks like a dead cow
It sounds like someone going away
It feels like falling off a wall.

Gary Cunningham (8)
St Mary's Primary School, Maghera

My Pet

My favourite pet is a dog,
I have a dog called Minnie.
I walk her every day.
I like my dog because she is good.
I take her to the beach,
I throw a stick,
She brings it back,
Then I give her a bit of food.
I like my dog because she is nice,
I will never give her away,
Until she is old and then,
I will have to take her to the pound,
I will be sad and so will my family.
When she had puppies she almost died,
The best pup of them all died.
But my grandad got a dog like mine.

Paul Stewart (11)
St Paul's Primary School, Slievemore

The Sun

The sun shines bright,
But it's not there at night,
It cannot melt water,
But it can melt snow as we know.

Flowers, seeds and plants grow,
As the sun shines, it's what we all know.
Through the summer the sun's always here,
To make us warm and full of cheer.

We'll go to the beach and paddle our feet,
But the sun's heat makes us fall asleep,
So we drink plenty of water to keep us on our feet,
So we enjoy the sun and eat some sweets.

Nicole McCloskey (10)
St Paul's Primary School, Slievemore

Summer

I like it in the summer
When the days are long and bright.
When we all sit in the garden
Or play in the evening light.

I like the scent of the flowers,
And the smell of the freshly cut grass
Or watching the little insects,
The butterflies, the bees and the wasps.

Riding on my bike,
I travel to the park
To play on the swings and roundabout,
Returning home before it's dark.

We all go to the seaside
And play in the water and the sand
Or climb upon the rocks
And gaze across the land.

Bobbie-Leigh Kelly (9)
St Paul's Primary School, Slievemore

The Playground

Out in our playground
We go each day
We run around
And we love to play

I play with my friends
We play tig
Then we run after each other
We all have fun.

Caolan Robinson (8)
St Paul's Primary School, Slievemore

My Dog Buddy

My dog Buddy is always in the muck,
He sometimes manages to get good luck.
When he was in an awful fight,
I saw him give a fearsome bite.

My dog Buddy is very strong,
He has a tail that is very long.
He can run very fast,
He was very small in the past.

Buddy is a talented dog,
He can easily get lost deep in the fog.
He can sit, he can lie,
If he was good we would bake him a pie.

Buddy's fur is golden-brown,
When I tell him, he just lies down.
When he's out he always get muddy,
He's my best friend, he's my dog *Buddy!*

Liam McDevitt (9)
St Paul's Primary School, Slievemore

The Playground

Children sitting on the benches
Writing, drawing, reading too
Kicking, punching, fighting
You'll want to be as good as me.

And picking leaves off the trees
Asking supervisors to understand
And I go out to the playground
With my friends to play games.

Jumping up and down
Falling to the ground
Then I put on my golden crown
And we play football against the wall.

Dayle King (9)
St Paul's Primary School, Slievemore

Holidays

I love going on my holidays,
It is such fun,
Going in the swimming pool,
And lying in the sun.

I love going on my holidays,
It is so cool,
So jump up and say, 'Hooray,
We're off school.'

I love going on my holidays,
Going out and dancing at nights,
And going round seeing beautiful sights.

I hate coming back from my holidays,
It is so sad,
Because the weather in Derry
Is really bad.

Alisha Belgrave (11)
St Paul's Primary School, Slievemore

The Playground

Children are chasing the ball around,
We are all running after the boys.
When it is raining we all stay in.
Something is slimy, it is a bug.

Some people play hopscotch,
We all play races
And we all play hopping
But when we fight, we make friends.

Boys and girls go chasing each other,
When I go out I play with my friends.
Sometimes we sit on the benches
Out in our playground.

Aoife Curran (8)
St Paul's Primary School, Slievemore

My Family

To me my mum is just the best,
She's better than all the rest.
All my friends think she's so cool,
She even wants a swimming pool.

To me my dad is very strong,
Even though he can do wrong,
I love my dad and always will,
But I think he needs a chill pill.

My brother Andrew fries my head,
If he hits me he gets sent to bed.
He'll come back down and say he's sorry,
But he'll hit me again like a big tough lorry.

My little sister can be good,
Tomato soup is her favourite food.
One of her fears are big, scary dogs,
And she loves to climb on big brown logs.

Shauna-Marie Stanway (11)
St Paul's Primary School, Slievemore

The Playground

Out in our playground
We go each day.
We run around
And we love to play.

We play football each day,
We run up to each net,
We try to score a goal
But if we don't score we lose.

David Houston (8)
St Paul's Primary School, Slievemore

Seasons

Spring is a time of flowers blooming,
All the drummers are blooming,
All the lambs are jumping about,
Children always shouting out.

Summer is a time of fun,
People lying in the sun,
Children playing all day,
People fishing at the bay.

Autumn is a time to chill,
The crazy people take a pill,
Children start dressing up,
Someone dressed up as a pup.

Winter is a time of joy,
Children playing with a new toy,
Children playing in the snow,
Someone said, 'Ho, ho, ho!'

Arón Halsey (11)
St Paul's Primary School, Slievemore

Roy Keane

My favourite player is the super Roy Keane,
He's a really good player and also a bit mean.
He makes a lot of tackles and always goes in hard,
He shouts at referees who sometimes gives a red card.

He's the captain of Man Utd, the best team in the land,
We are going to win the Premiership if Roy doesn't get banned.
I really love it when he plays for the men in green,
Because Roy's a superstar, super Roy Keane.

Aaron Robinson (10)
St Paul's Primary School, Slievemore

Ronaldinho

Ronaldinho is my favourite player,
Even though he has long curly hair.
Ronaldinho plays football with a smile on his face,
He leaves defenders behind with his pace.

Ronaldinho is a coloured man,
I'll always be his number one fan.
When he runs with the ball at his feet,
All you can hear is the Barcelona beat.

One day at the Brandywell I saw him play,
I wish I could see him every day.
Barcelona beat Derry by a mile,
The man with the long curly hair made the fans smile.

I'm a keeper and I would be full of fear,
If Ronaldinho came anywhere near.
I am now coming to the end of my poem,
Ronaldinho and I are now away home.

Patrick Quigley (10)
St Paul's Primary School, Slievemore

The Playground

Out in our playground,
We go each day,
We run and shout, 'Hooray,'
And we pretend to fight.

Out in our playground,
We play games and run,
We play dancing and skipping,
We all have such fun.

Out in our playground,
We play each day,
When we get hurt we sit down,
And get a plaster put on us.

Kevin Harrison (8)
St Paul's Primary School, Slievemore

The Seasons!

Spring, summer
Autumn, winter
Are the seasons
Of the year.

Spring is the season
When buds form on trees
When lambs and foals are born
Summertime is a happy time
For playing games and having fun
For relaxing on the beach
And watching the sun go down
Autumn time turns leaves
Red, orange, yellow and brown

It's harvest time and crops are getting harvested
Wintertime, the trees are bare
Hedgehogs, squirrels and dormice
Are hibernating under leaves and trees
Christmas time is coming.

Now you've heard about the seasons
Spring, summer
Autumn, winter
Which is your favourite?
Mine is winter.

Denise Coyle (10)
St Paul's Primary School, Slievemore

My Family

My mammy is small and nice
She works all through the day and all night
Her food is very nice, she makes it every day for me
She could do it for someone else but instead she does it for me.

My daddy is tall and very nice
He works in a big factory
He has hair and blue eyes
I love my daddy, he means everything to me.

My brother is stupid
He's very annoying, he fights with me
And pulls my hair and hits me every day
Every morning he comes into my room and hits me
Then I get up and batter him
But I love my brother.

My baby sister is really nice
She has long brown hair and bright blue eyes
But sometimes she can be very annoying
I play with her every day
I love my little sister.

Rachel Kelly (10)
St Paul's Primary School, Slievemore

Going Fishing

Searching for worms
Digging for sod
Off to the Foyle
With my fishing rod.

Watching the water
Peaceful and still
Making a fire
If we've time to kill.

Searching our bags
Ready to munch
Biscuits and crisps
We call it lunch.

I look at my watch
It's getting dark
What a day I had
With my big brother Mark.

Máelán Brennán (10)
St Paul's Primary School, Slievemore

My Little Nieces And Nephews

My little niece is called Aoife
She thinks she is a diva
She is a little pest
She thinks she is better than all the rest.

My little nephew is called Shea
And I think he was born to play
He is really fun
And he hates the sun.

I have a nephew, Bailey
And he batters you daily
He has red hair
And he loves his teddy bear.

My brother's wife just had a baby
It is already driving me crazy
Her name is Patrice
She is my new little niece.

My nieces and nephews are really fun
And I thank God for every one.

Erin McGowan (10)
St Paul's Primary School, Slievemore

Chirpy!

My bird Chirpy looked like a very playful and colourful bird,
He was really a cockatiel
And loved to whistle
The tunes my dad taught him
But he did make up his own too.

Chirpy had spiky white and grey hair,
A yellow face with rosy-red cheeks,
He also had a grey and white body,
With a small yellow and orange beak and feet,
His beak and claws were big, really big.

I liked Chirpy,
He was really my true, best friend,
I miss him now because he died a year ago,
I wish he was here with me now,
I miss him a lot and deep inside
I really loved him.

Bronagh Quigley (11)
St Paul's Primary School, Slievemore

My Favourite Footballer

My favourite footballer is Thierry Henry,
He has lots of skill.
He scores a lot of goals,
He plays for Arsenal.

He used to be no good,
But now he is a five star player.
A whole lots of goals Henry has,
He has 63 goals in the Premiership.

One of his friends is Viera,
Viera is his friend because he's from France.
He is a five star midfielder,
And he plays for Arsenal.

Henry is very good,
He eats less food.
What if Henry scores a goal,
Then is hit by a pole.

Andrew Quigley (10)
St Paul's Primary School, Slievemore

Cats

I have a cat named Vinny,
Who has a magpie friend,
They are best of friends,
But sometimes they drive each other round the bend.

When I am in bed at night,
He pushes me left to right,
And when I'm on the phone,
I give him an ice cream bone.

When they go to parties,
They eat lot of Smarties,
And when they come back, they are drunk,
So they get a big thump.

Emer Lowry (8)
Termoncanice Primary School

Night

All of a sudden he will appear,
Trapping you in a corner,
Trembling with fear.

This man has no family,
No father or mother,
As he draws closer,
You begin to shudder.

For this man's problem there is no cure,
The pain and suffering,
He has to endure.

On us he takes out the anger he sparks,
Leaving with us nothing,
But dark.

Sean Og O'Hara (11)
Termoncanice Primary School

Night

Night is a fierce animal,
She makes me feel terrified,
Her face looks like a black cave,
Her hair is long and flowing,
Her clothes are lined with jewels
Which sparkle in the night.
When she moves, she moves swiftly and silently.
Her voice is the hoot of an owl or the howl of a wolf.
Her mouth is gaping and gobbles up the world.
She lives in a deep, dark cave with the bats and badgers.
Night frightens me!

Kathryn McShane (10)
Termoncanice Primary School

The Football Pitch

Nasty tackling,
Supporters cheering,
Teams scoring,
Rain pouring,
Players dribbling,
Substitutes running,
Supporters singing,
The whistle's blowing,
Aah! We've lost the match!

Paul Eakin (7)
Termoncanice Primary School

My Poem

Christmas is fun
Christmas is great
It is the birth of Jesus
That's why we celebrate

I like Christmas films
I like Christmas lights
I like Christmas presents
And even Christmas night.

Kevin Martin (9)
Termoncanice Primary School

Hallowe'en

Hallowe'en is great
It is really fun
I have a little golden ball, I use it for my beat
And when the sun comes back up I'll fly away back to Mum.

Katie Guy (9)
Termoncanice Primary School

Dragons

Dragons may be extinct,
But you can have your say,
You've got to stop and think,
So you can vote your way.

Vote for dragons, they're alive,
You should see their features,
Of course they live,
They're in every reptile creature.

Dragons have enormous wings,
They're not like snakes or frogs,
They use their wings to spring,
And they are carnivores like dogs.

That's the end of discussion, they're alive,
So leave the scientists alone,
Maybe, you don't think they live,
Oh no, the dragon's starting to groan.

Hannah McDonald (9)
Termoncanice Primary School

Zoo'ing' Poem

Lions roaring,
Tigers pounding,
Elephants stamping,
Kangaroos hopping,
Giraffes munching,
Pandas crunching,
Cheetahs speeding,
Rhinos rampaging,
Parrots squawking,
Leopards sneaking,
Warthogs snorting,
Hyenas grinning,
Now we're leaving!

Joe McNerlin (8)
Termoncanice Primary School

Be Friends

A friend is someone whom you can trust
You always, always, always must
Have at least one friend
Because the friendship you have will never end.

Friendship is the best thing ever
You must never, never, never, never
Fight with someone - anyone
Then you won't be friends with that special someone.

Friends are gentle, generous and kind
Sometimes stop and think in your mind
Should I do this, should I do that?
Oh no! I did the wrong thing, drat!

In the playground join in, have fun
Then you'll feel like you are number one
I hope you decide not to bully
Then your happiness will grow fully.

Cliodhna McIlvenny (8)
Termoncanice Primary School

A Spot Of Colour

White is the colour of the moon dazzling in the night sky,
A piece of paper just waiting to be drawn on,
Clouds peaceful, floating in the sky,
Freshly fallen snow at Christmas time.

Red is the colour of a newborn baby's rosy cheeks,
Of a red-breasted robin on a summer's day,
Of a rosy red, red rose gently flowing in the wind.

Yellow is the colour of a dandelion flowing in the breeze,
Homer in The Simpsons saying, 'D'oh!'
The sun blazing in the sky.

Kate McManus (8)
Termoncanice Primary School

Colour Poem

White is . . .
The colour of snow falling from the sky
Building the snowman way up high
A swan swimming down the lake
The white clouds up in the sky.

Red is . . .
The colour of a robin's red breast
Roses blooming in the summer
A red fox hunting for food at night
The colour of my heart beating inside me.

Yellow is . . .
The colour of a lemon sitting in a fruit bowl
And the sun up in the big blue sky
Daffodils sitting in my garden during the summer
Sand in the beach being built into a sandcastle.

Ciaran Mullan (9)
Termoncanice Primary School

Bright Colour Poem

Red is the colour of a juicy strawberry,
Red feels like wobbly jelly,
Red smells like a sweet rose on a summer's day.

Yellow is the colour of a sour lemon,
Yellow tastes like a big banana,
Yellow daffodils shine in the sun.

White is the colour of snow,
White is Santa's beard on Christmas night,
White milk from a cow put into bottles,
White as a fluffy cloud floating in the sky.

Emma Mullan (9)
Termoncanice Primary School

Colour Poem

Yellow is . . .
The colour of ripe corn swaying in the breeze,
The sun shining in the blue sky on a summer's day,
A juicy melon in a fruit shop,
A light on a winter's night.

Red is . . .
The colour of a robin's breast,
My cheeks when I run in cross-country,
A rose blooming in the spring,
A fox's tail swishing about.

White is . . .
The colour of snow in the winter,
As bright as the stars at night,
As shiny as the frames in my window,
As white as milk that comes from a cow.

Christopher Trainer (9)
Termoncanice Primary School

Colour Poem

White is the colour of snow floating in the air
Milk on a frosty doorstep
Sugar in my tea
A white board at school.

Red is the colour of my homework book
Like a rose
Like blood flowing out of a knee
Like a red pen on a page.

Yellow is the colour of the sun in the sky
Like the colour yellow in a rainbow
Like a book
Like the light on the roof.

Michael Quigley (8)
Termoncanice Primary School

Friends

Friends, friends, you need them all,
Even when you're playing ball,
No matter what they look like,
Or if their name is Mike.

Always keep a friend in mind,
Where you may be,
No matter if they're kind or not,
Or if they eat the fleas.

Try not to lose a friend,
Or you'll end up being lonely,
So try to be kind,
Even if you have only one.

I'm sure they'll keep you in mind!

Gemma Harbinson (9)
Termoncanice Primary School

A Verse Of Colour

The colour of her wedding dress is sparkling white,
Her crown gleams with the sunlight,
'They are the right couple for each other,'
I heard my mum say in a soft, gentle whisper.

There is a family of roses in my garden,
My mum comes out every sunny morning and says, 'Mmm.'
I plant more every day and water them,
My roses are very pleasant to smell.

The colour of the sun is a bright yellow colour,
It is the hottest ball in space,
I really want to visit it but I don't want to die,
I run outside on a sunny day and I guess I'm stuck on Earth.

Niamh McVeigh (8)
Termoncanice Primary School

Rhyming Poem

White is the colour of falling snow
Then it lies on the ground
Till it melts very slow,
Nice to see it come and go.

Red is the colour of a juicy apple,
When I bite into it the juice runs down my chin.
Sometimes the skin gets stuck in my teeth,
I might have one now.

Yellow is the colour of the bright yellow sun
If you go up to the sky you will see it glow.
I want to visit the sun
But I guess I'm stuck on Earth.

Megan McLaughlin (8)
Termoncanice Primary School

A Drop Of Colour

Yellow is a bright star in a clear night
A daffodil spreading its petals
Gold, sparkling non-stop when you see it
The sun shining on a clear day, on a summer day.

Green is the colour of grass in your garden
Apples in the orchard, nice and juicy
Leaves on a plant in a big and wide field
Peas in a shop freshly picked.

Red is like a fire on Guy Fawkes night
A nice sunset to end the day
A strawberry in a fruit bowl inside our house
Foxes in their den sleeping softly.

Rory Squires (9)
Termoncanice Primary School

Colours

White is the colour of the great, fluffy clouds
On a beautiful summer's day.
White is the great blanket of snow
Which covers the ground.
White is the colour of a delicate snowdrop.

Yellow is the colour of the sun shining so bright
High in the sky, so hot in the sky,
Oh! I need a drink!
The sun is bright, bright, bright.

Red is the colour of a bright red rose
Sitting in a garden of roses.
Sitting and showing off their colours.
Roses are showing their long stems,
Red roses are very red.

Ashley McLean (9)
Termoncanice Primary School

Colour Poem - White

White is the colour of fresh cold milk,
A snowman as cold as can be,
A cloud drifting around the sky,
A piece of paper straight from a pack.

White is the colour of pale sick faces,
A white board that you can write on,
The opposite of black is white,
Paper plates with crimps.

White is the colour of clean tissues,
A polystyrene ball,
Fluffy, puffy cotton wool,
Ice cream that is vanilla flavour.

Ciara Robertson (9)
Termoncanice Primary School

Colour Poems

White is . . .
The colour of this page I write on
The snow as it falls down
White are the clouds in the sky
The milk in my cornflakes.

Red is . . .
The colour of raspberries waiting to be picked
As red as a Man Utd T-shirt as they walk away
It is the colour of my schoolbag as I walk away
A colour of a robin's breast as it flies away.

Yellow is . . .
The colour of the sun as it shines in the day
It's the colour of daffodils as they grow
It is the colour of my pencil that I write with
It is the colour of the juicy lemon I eat.

Adam Mullan (9)
Termoncanice Primary School

Colour

Red is the colour of a clown's nose twirling around the stage
Or an animal sitting on a page
Also a red monster munching all the way.

White is the colour of snow lying on the ground
Like a carpet of ice cream in the winter
Snowflakes fluttering onto the ground
Milk pouring onto cereals.

Yellow is the colour of butter onto toast
And a buttercup glistening all the way
Like the sun shining on all the building tops.

Kathryn O'Connor (9)
Termoncanice Primary School

Favourite Things

One of my favourite things is my pet
He is really fluffy
That's something to bet
And I wonder if his fluff is stuffy?

Another of my favourite things is food,
Breakfast, lunch and dinner
My mum and dad cook very good
They're the best, they're winners!

Another is my friends,
I can talk to them on the phone
Or write letters to send
You can even have a four-legged one
That eats a bone

Home is another
I really like my bed
Home is good without a brother
Or by now I'd be dead.

Traci Adams (8)
Termoncanice Primary School

Cross-Country

I love to do cross-country
It really is good fun
It's great when I come first
I like to do it in the sun.

It really is quite painful
I don't know how I pull it off
But when I am near the end
I badly need to cough.

Patrick McCloskey (9)
Termoncanice Primary School

A Poem About Colours

Green is the colour of a freshly picked apple from the orchard
Grass in the garden
Cabbages in the cabbage patch
Pears from the fruit bowl

White is the colour of whipped cream
Clouds floating by
Milk from the milkman's cart
Paper which we write on.

Yellow is the colour of the sun on a hot day
Butter spread on toast
Chicks hatching from eggs
Buttercups on a summer's day.

Matthew O'Connor (8)
Termoncanice Primary School

Favourite Things

My favourite things,
Many people have them,
Some have one,
Some have two,
Some maybe have three.
I have two,
My brother has one.
My favourite thing is a bike,
I ride my bike along the shore,
My brother at my side,
We go in search of ice cream
To cool us in the melting sun.

Myra Kate Feeney (8)
Termoncanice Primary School

Young Writers - Playground Poets Co Londonderry

My Poem

She laughs and giggles
She's full of life too
She loves the attention
She tries anything that is new
She thinks I might as well try it
It might taste good
You never know
I'll try it anyway, I think she should.

Emma Kelly (9)
Termoncanice Primary School

Monster

When I woke, I got quite a fright
The monster was mad and crazy
As I saw him through the dungeon light,
I guess he was a long way away,
But later on that night
As I was having my tea
I mumbled to myself, 'W-w-what is it?'
Then I thought, *it's the monster!*

Jack Deery (8)
Termoncanice Primary School

My Pet Monster

My pet is scary and creepy
He wakes me up in the middle of the night
Giving me a terrible fright
He's black and blue and stripy too
He even scares my mummy too.

Jordan Fleming (9)
Termoncanice Primary School

Zoo'ing' Poem

Lions roaring and pouncing.
Rhinoceros stampeding and charging.
Giraffes stretching, eating and sleeping.
Ground mole popping.
Kangaroos hopping.
Elephants earthquaking.
Eagles flying and preying.
Piranhas scrambling and eating.
Zookeeper locking.

Conor O'Neill (7)
Termoncanice Primary School

Colour Poem

White is the colour of snowflakes
Milk on a frosty doorstep
A snowman with hat and scarf.

Red is the colour of roses growing in the summer
Roses are beautiful and smell nice in summer.

Yellow is the colour of the sun
In the morning's bright and beautiful sky.

Daniel Moran (9)
Termoncanice Primary School

My Family

I like my family because they care,
They remind me of a big fat bear.
When you meet they'll talk about me,
So come on over and you will see.

Shannon McAteer (9)
Termoncanice Primary School

Babies

Children are nice, children are sweet
But please keep them quiet
Not under our feet.

Babies are now in bed
I can rest my sore head
I am going to take off my shoes
And have a little snooze.

It is morning when I wake
I haven't time for a break
The children go to school
And now I am feeling cool.

Beth Burridge   (9)
Termoncanice Primary School

Animals

I like animals
I like them so much
I like their feelings
I like their touch
Animals, animals, I like them so much.

Lauren Kelly (8)
Termoncanice Primary School

Horse Riding

Horse riding is fun
The jumping is the best
When I'm riding I have a smile
And take off to the west.

Rebecca Henry (9)
Termoncanice Primary School

My Aunt

I have the best aunt,
She makes me lovely food,
She shows me how to make things
Which I think is really good,
Her name is Julie-Ann and she really is quite pretty,
She tells me lots of funny things,
So she's also very witty.

Thea McCloskey (9)
Termoncanice Primary School

Ruud Van Nistelrooy

Nistelrooy, oh Nistelrooy, you sure show that ball,
All those boys are no match at all,
When you score your team is so, so, so, so glad,
But for the other team they get so, so mad.

When you're on the field you have so much skill,
I just know you'll score a goal, I just know you will,
That other goalie doesn't stand a chance
'Cause when you're on the field you're in a sort of trance.

Nistelrooy keep on track, stop looking at your wife,
Keep staying on track, she'll still be there when you get back.

Ryan Campbell (9)
Termoncanice Primary School

My Poem

My favourite colour is red,
At 8pm I go to bed.
I get up in the morning for school,
And after school I go to the pool.
In the evening I get my dinner,
And at the end of the day I am the winner.

Chloe Pearson (9)
Termoncanice Primary School

Rhyming Poem

The white clouds go sailing by
Away up high in the sky.
The little white house on the hill
Stands alone and so still.

Yellow is the colour of a juicy lemon
Coming out of the fridge
And like the hot sun on a summer's day
And everywhere you go.

Amyleigh O'Connor (9)
Termoncanice Primary School

Chocolate

Chocolate, chocolate in my tummy
It really tastes very yummy
I like to eat it every day
My favourite of all is Milky Way.

There's Aero, Bounty and Galaxy too
All these bars I love to chew
Turkish delight and lovely Milk Tray
But best of all is Milky Way.

Niamh Feeney (9)
Termoncanice Primary School

White

White is the colour of snow drifting down from the sky,
It is the colour of fresh milk fresh from a cow.
The colour of a cloud drifting in the sky.
White is the colour of a seagull at the seaside,
A white piece of paper in a book,
A white ice cream for you and me to enjoy by the sea.

Nicole McGillion (9)
Termoncanice Primary School

A Housey Mousey Rap

My big brother owns a big house,
My little brother is a dumb mouse
And I'm a boy
Who was a toy.

I go down a sewer to find my brother
But I can't find him so I go down another,
Then I find him in a gutter,
Eating a little bit of butter.

I go to my brother's house
But my big brother finds out he's a woodlouse
I take him to the doctors to get a treat,
After that we have some meat.

We go to the house and get some supper
Then we go to the gym and get a lot tougher
After that we have a bit of fun,
When we get back home the world is done.

Daniel Forrest (9)
Termoncanice Primary School

The Colour White

White is the colour of milk.
Milk on a frosty doorstep.
The moon shining at night
When werewolves are growling.

White roses are my favourite
They look so pretty in the light.
I wish I had some right now.
My mummy likes them in the light.

A polar bear has white fur.
We wear fur in the winter.
I have a fur coat, I wear it.
It looks so pretty.

Saoirse Mullan (9)
Termoncanice Primary School

Cristiano Ronaldo

Ronaldo, he is magic
He wears a magic hat
And when he saw Old Trafford
He said, 'I fancy that!'

He didn't sign for Arsenal or Chelsea
Cos there'd be a fight
He signed for Man United
Cos they're really dynamite.

When you score a goal
You celebrate like mad
And all the rest of the team
Are really, really glad.

Ruairi Hassan (9)
Termoncanice Primary School

The Lion

The lion, the lion he jumps into bed
He wriggles and giggles
And hits me on the head.
Sometimes he snores,
Sometimes he roars
And I always have to close the doors.

My mum wakes up in the morning and moans
'Get rid of that lion that moans and groans.'
Once I said, *'No!'*
Then I said, *'Yes!'*
So we got rid of the lion and Mum said, 'Poor you.'
But then I realised he would be better in the *zoo!*

Correy Feeney (9)
Termoncanice Primary School

My Best Friend

His name is Michael
We play football every day
He's generous and kind
In every way.

He likes horses and bugs
We drink hot chocolate out of little mugs
We always have some fun
We always have a chocolate bun.

Lewis Donaghy (9)
Termoncanice Primary School

My Pet

My pet is a cat,
My cat lies on the mat,
My cat plays with wool,
My cat is a fool.

The cat I have is very sad
And he is very bad,
The cat plays with me,
The cat chases some bees.

Catherine Carlin Moore (9)
Termoncanice Primary School

My Best Friend

Melissa is my friend,
A very nice one too
She's got long black, curly hair
Even including brown skin and eyes
Melissa has a gym in her house,
She even has pretty saris
Melissa is special to me in every way.

Rosie Forrest (8)
Termoncanice Primary School

A Tiger

A tiger has sharp teeth,
He eats all the leaves,
Everyone thinks he's a thief,
The tiger's name is Keith

He lives in a jungle
He is very fast,
He loves his little story called Mungle,
He never wants to be last.

Roisin Turner (9)
Termoncanice Primary School

Lions

They're cool and cunning,
They're very hairy
And they're fast at running,
They're very, very, very *scary!*

They're not very quiet,
They like to roar,
They like to make riots
And they love to *snore!*

Alice McGee (9)
Termoncanice Primary School

Raindrops Of Colour

Red is the colour of a juicy red apple on a hot summer day.
Red is thick, thick dark blood.
Red is a thorn in a country garden.

Yellow is the colour of a star in the night sky.
A bright, hot sun.
A sour lemon that makes your eyes water.

Matthew Simpson (8)
Termoncanice Primary School

Colours Of The World

Green is the colour of the nice grass shining in the sun
Of a frog hopping in the air,
The fresh apple sitting in the fruit bowl,
The leaves fluttering down from the treetops.

Red is the colour of a strawberry lying in the fruit bowl,
The colour of my homework book,
The apple high up in the tree,
A big ball of fire coming right at you.

Blue is the colour of the sea shining up at me,
The colour of the salty sea shining up to the sky,
The sky shining down on everybody.

Yellow is the colour of the lovely melon sitting in the fruit bowl,
The sun blazing down,
The butter sitting in the fridge to be put on toast.

Aaron Mullan (9)
Termoncanice Primary School

Sea 'ing' Poem

Waves are swaying,
Fishes swimming,
Octopus laughing,
Mermaids dancing,
Crabs scuttling,
Mermen muttering,
Seaweed fluttering,
Seagulls flying,
Sea sweeping,
Dolphins jumping,
Sun is setting,
Stars are twinkling,
Moon is shining.

Maria McQuillan (8)
Termoncanice Primary School

Colour Poem

White is the colour of clouds in the sky,
Milk on a frosty doorstep
And in all the boxes,
A white horse in the field

Yellow is the colour of the sun in the sky,
Our school's home diary,
A yellow display on the wall,
Stars in the sky shining.

Red is the colour of the sunset in the nice night,
A red Coke can in the shop,
Roses on the ground,
A red box in the shop.

Seamus O'Hara (9)
Termoncanice Primary School

A Fish's Wish

I had a fish,
That wanted a wish.
I gave it a pebble,
Then it trebled.

I gave it a castle
But the fish was baffled.
I gave it a broom,
It thought I was a prune.

Finally I gave it the last thing I had,
All except the food.
Oh, aren't I rude,
All it wanted was just food.

Mark Gormley (9)
Termoncanice Primary School

Lots Of Colour

Red is the colour of a nice red rose,
Hot red lava that will burn my clothes.
It's the colour of a Malteser box
And the warm soft coat of the cunning fox.

Yellow is the colour of an old man's teeth,
A nice crispy, yellow, autumn leaf.
It is also the colour of a nice sunflower
And a ripe lemon that's really sour.

White is the colour of cold, cold snow
And washing powder that is a dirty germ's foe.
White is the colour of clouds in the sky
And freshly whipped cream on a nice big pie.

Conor Murphy (9)
Termoncanice Primary School

Colour Poem

Red is the colour of
A lovely juicy apple in the orchard.
Cranberry juice I drink with my dinner.
A beautiful sunset sky up in Cruit Island.

White is the colour of
White clouds drifting across on a summer's day.
Snow on the ground covering everything.
A girl wearing a white dress on a beautiful day.

Yellow is the colour of
A lovely melon when I taste it.
Sun in the morning when it comes up on a lovely day.
Daffodils growing in the springtime.

Aoife Murray (9)
Termoncanice Primary School

Jess The Dog

My lovely dog Jess is soft and furry
The only problem is she's always in a hurry.

Sometimes I think my dog can talk
When she goes to the door looking for a walk.

When I wake she licks my face
When I'm asleep she eats my lace.

My dog is happy when wagging her tail
While waiting on the postman to deliver the mail.

Blaine Ferris (8)
Termoncanice Primary School

My Dog

My dog, he is so funny.
He is full of sweet, sweet honey.
He is so furry and likes Chinese curry
And when you see him he's in a hurry.

Paul McLaughlin (9)
Termoncanice Primary School

Trapped

As I sit in a cage
I see some birds fly
There is no escape in my cage
I try to see why
But then I hear it opening
Thank you! Thank you!
I am a bird.

Stephen McDermott (10)
Trench Road Primary School

Trapped

I'm trapped here
All alone
Waiting for
Another one
To come and save me
From this cage
Voices are going
Around my head
I dream about
Being free
But please I beg
Somebody save me.

Eve Hinds (10)
Trench Road Primary School

Trapped

When I sit at the bottom of the sea
Lying still in a colourful shell
I am lonely as I sit.
The dolphin has me in his mouth
And throws me on the beach.
A little girl picks me up
Her favourite colour is pink
As that's the colour I am
Oh why?
Yes, I am a little pink pearl.

Danielle Moran (10)
Trench Road Primary School

Hated - Haiku

Why do they hate me?
I am alone in the dark,
Please someone save me!

Dearbháile McKinney (11)
Trench Road Primary School

Reading - Haiku

Read books and enjoy
Mysterious, fictional,
Entertaining too.

Sophie Moore (11)
Trench Road Primary School

Trapped

A prison cell dull and grey
Bare walls I see every day
I sit down anchored to the ground
Ball and chain hold me down.
The musty smell
I feel like puking
So cold and lonely
Nothing to do except sit around
Bad thoughts in my head
While people scream and shout
I feel so trapped
Wouldn't you?

Joseph McDermott (10)
Trench Road Primary School

Horse Riding - Haiku

Fun, grooming, saddle
Walking, trotting, cantering
Rusty is my friend.

Jane Doherty (10)
Trench Road Primary School

Trapped!

Underground, squashed, dirty,
Dark and cold
I want to just burst out
Instead of being
Cold and damp and lonely
I am waiting for spring
Waiting for the birds to chirp
The sign to bloom.
Colourful, beautiful
And a lovely smell.
The winter has passed
I have heard the tune
From the birds
Here I am! Watch out!
Here I am
A beautiful
Flower!

Kevin Harkin (9)
Trench Road Primary School

Trapped

I'm trapped,
trapped in a cage,
something walking around
ready to jump at me,
but I'll get them if I escape,
but it's something scary,
something hunting me.
I think it's a white ape
or maybe more.
God help me,
I'm just a little monkey
lonely and scared in a cage.

Dearbhla Tunney (9)
Trench Road Primary School

Trapped

Pawing around my cage,
Hearing gasps and oohs,
Tasting fear,
Seeing people happy,
But I'm not happy,
In captivity.
I'll dazzle them
With my black and orange stripes.
Ugly faces looking in at me,
Monotonously tramping this cage,
Day after day . . .

Bronagh Brolly (9)
Trench Road Primary School

People - Haiku

Generous people,
Caring, loving and laughing
Tall, skinny people.

Sinead Meenan (11)
Trench Road Primary School

The Sea - Haiku

Crashing, eroding
Hitting off the hard, hard rocks
Thundering, splashing.

Siofra Coyle (11)
Trench Road Primary School

Books

Books, books, I can't live without books,
It's better than that unintelligent television,
You'd simply know a lot more,
But everyone thinks it's a bore,
Except for comics,
Those boring old comics!
I'm into adventure and mysteries
And I like climbing trees,
But nothing could be better,
Oh nothing could be better,
Than books!

Enya McGlinchey (9)
Trench Road Primary School

Filipino - Haiku

Different language,
My native spoken wording,
Always makes me laugh.

Jorel B Bautista (11)
Trench Road Primary School

The Sea - Haiku

The sea is crawling
With fishes of many kinds
Beautiful fish glow.

Eoin Farrelly (10)
Trench Road Primary School

Wake Up To No Smoking

Wake up to no smoking
If you don't you'll be choking.

W hen you go smoking
A lways you'll come home choking
K ill the fag not yourself
E veryone can make a choice

U ttering around you are the people who hate smoking
P ersonally I think it's disgusting

T errorising people who don't like smoking
O dours will come from your breath

N ever smoke! Get my point
O utstanding numbers of people die from it each year

S o you have a choice
M ake the wrong one, death
O r make the right one, quit smoking
K eep using patches and nicotine gum
I n a while you'll stop
N ow make the right choice
G et those fags in the bin.

Dearbháil Gillespie (11)
Trench Road Primary School

Trapped

As I sit alone
children passing by my window
make me feel very young again.
Children laughing and having fun
make me want to get out of my seat again.

Darren Devine (10)
Trench Road Primary School